What It Takes to be Successful in B2B, You Learned In

Kindergarten

By Duane H. Cook

2010 Edition

Blogs...Collaboration...EDI...Email...eMarkets...Exchange...
Kindles...Tweets...Websites...Wiki...

The technology doesn't matter.

The soft skills behind the technology are what makes for
successful Business to Business. It is often the last thing
considered when putting up a technology driven
application....and it is always the key determinate for
success or failure.

You already possess what is needed for success. You
learned it in Kindergarten.

FOR INFORMATION (INCLUDING SPECIAL MARKETS PURCHASES FOR EDUCATIONAL, BUSINESS, OR SALE PROMOTION USE) ADDRESS TO

Strategic
eBusiness
C⬤OK
CONSULTING

53 County Clare Crescent, Fairport, NY 14450

COOK, DUANE H. (DUANE HAROLD), 1951-
WHAT IT TAKES TO BE SUCCESSFUL IN B2B, YOU LEARNED IN KINDERGARTEN. – 2010 EDITION

FIRST EDITION UNITED STATES COPYRIGHT CERTIFICATION OF REGISTRATION NUMBER: TXU1-195-263

Library of Congress Control Number: 2010900371
ISBN-10: 1450507697
ISBN-13/EAN-13: 9781450507691

BISAC CATEGORY: BUSINESS & ECONOMICS / E-COMMERCE / GENERAL

*To the best kindergarten teacher ever –
my sister, Dorothea*

Table of Contents

Introduction

This book is not the "Dummy's Guide to B2B," just as kindergarten is not for dummies.

This book is for those of us who listened to all the technical advice, put together our web applications, played by all the rules-- and then were still disappointed by the results.

It's for those of us who watched all those IBM and Microsoft advertisements-- and didn't think B2B could possibly be this hard.

It's for those of us who think we must have done something wrong. For those of us who think, "I must be the only one who doesn't get it."

It's for those in the frustrating middle of the corporation, watching our companies plod along with unsatisfactory eBusiness results due to a lack of vision at the top.

It's for those of us who feel helpless or hapless.

It's for those of us who are discouraged and don't know how to get things started-- or restarted.

Social First

I will always remember my twin sister and me on the front porch at home before our first day of kindergarten. Our nametags and important enrollment papers were firmly attached to our shirts with safety pins. My hair was slicked down. We were wearing new "school clothes" and "school shoes." Mom took pictures, cried, kissed us, cried some more, and off we went.

We were less than twenty yards into our walk toward school before my sister needed to run back to the bathroom. I guess we were all nervous.

Once we were at school we were directed to the cafetorium, dutifully sorted out by helpful mothers and staff, and lined up in front of our teachers. Finally, we were marched single file into our classrooms. I will never forget the first time I saw my kindergarten classroom--the asphalt tile floor, the large throw rug and my teacher's rocking chair, where she would sit and read to us. We sat on the floor and anxiously awaited our first few minutes of school.

I was assigned to Miss Waters' class. No, it wasn't love at first sight: But it was close. Do all boys fall in love with their kindergarten teachers?

Our indoctrination was not about teaching us anything in particular. It was all about making us comfortable. We needed to understand the few basic rules; there would be much more to come later. We needed to know how to play well with each other, but most things could wait for another day. We needed to learn many things like writing and arithmetic, but all that would wait for another year.

First and foremost, right now, we needed to learn social skills for getting along with each other. We needed to establish trust with one another.

We need to put first things first. I have been involved with eBusiness for more years than I wish to count. It has always worked well when we have gotten first things first. The social before the technical. We rarely start with the social. Why is that?

eBusiness projects have a high mortality rate, but not for the reasons that come to us at first blush. I frequently encounter businesses or functional units that are so driven to "get their savings" that they forget that getting those savings depends upon putting first things first.

I cannot count the number of times I've seen businesses attempt to drive a trading partner to some solution. Usually, they puff up their chests and declare, "If they want to do business with us, they will do it our way." They lay out their technical requirements, plans, and schedules. They line up their pilot customers based on some elaborate formula to obtain the highest value in the shortest amount of time or with least effort. Hogwash!

Rarely does that work. Oh, it may work sometimes if you are the 800-pound gorilla. The Wal*Marts of the world can pull it off (or at least sometimes do). Not easily, however, even for them. And most of us aren't the 800-pound gorilla.

If you are the buyer in the relationship, you typically have more leverage. But usually not enough. I have seen every excuse in the book by suppliers and customers. I have seen every method imaginable employed to delay moving forward. Sometimes intentionally, other times unintentionally; sometimes for valid reasons, other times not. So much for "getting them to do it our way."

I have even seen more than one customer push aggressively to gain agreement to move forward only to be stopped cold in their tracks a few days later.

And I have seen three extremely successful eBusiness initiatives in my career; all three laid the correct foundation for being successful. All three were highly focused on the implementation phase from the customer's viewpoint. All three engaged customers early on in the process to understand their issues. All three had a high level of customer involvement and commitment. All three tested and retested their assumptions with the users to understand whether or not we were "on the mark."

None of these solutions utilized the latest, sexiest solutions. None of these had to wait for the next generation of technology solution and software. All three projects were hard work. All three were wildly successful, beyond our expectations. If anything, we were remiss in not expecting more of ourselves. All three put "first things first."

Unfortunately, we typically exhibit corporate amnesia. Corporate historians are few and far between. Usually we are in such a rush to get on with the next projects that we don't pass along the legacy of our journey. We don't typically create the forums in our companies to discuss our pain and suffering and share our successes. We fail to retain "knowledge management" of what works, and what doesn't. As a result, we exhibit corporate amnesia and the next group gets to learn the same lessons and endure the same pain. They get to risk failure and learn the lesson of "first things first" the hard way.

I am not talking about eliminating the learning curve; painful as it may be, most of us learn best from our mistakes. I am talking about reducing the learning curve on the initial pain points of our projects so that we can get deeper and deeper into our projects and learn new things that can be passed along to others. In other words, rushing to the next learning curve.

eBusiness is not a trail we travel by ourselves. Other than very limited internal B2E (Business to Employee) applications, most eBusiness applications involve parties outside our four walls (vendors or suppliers, customers, carriers, banks, etc.). Engaging those outside our organizations requires social skills-- the skills we learned in kindergarten. It requires getting into our trading partners' heads to understand their concerns, their visions, their desires, their passions, and their issues.

I have never been to a customer's site for an initial discussion of eBusiness where I didn't get blasted with the "issue du jour." These issues typically are not at the heart of their problems and never are based around my reason for being there. But you are the warm body that represents your company. Consider this your test. If you can help with that issue, no matter how off topic or sidetracked it may be, you get handed a chip. This is a trust chip. You will get to use that trust chip at some point. It may be when you need a favor from the customer in getting some phase of the project done. It may be used years later when the customer needs to make an investment and can't quite see the benefits of some activity. When you have earned your first trust chip, you have moved along the line of a successful implementation, and you may not have even gotten to the issue at hand.

"Socially comfortable" comes before "technology comfortable." The essential truth that we seem to always set aside is "high tech requires high touch." We need to nurture and help our trading partners through the transition to eBusiness. This is new territory for most people. Those of us who have successfully been down the rapids of eBusiness before need to assist others in their first journey. We need to recognize the inherent dangers and risks to them that are involved.

This requires a conscious decision on our part to dedicate the time and energy necessary to make others comfortable that the feelings and concerns they have are not only normal, but to be expected. The stark truth is that we need to love our trading partners enough to want them to succeed. We need to desire their success above our own.

eBusiness projects live and die, based on our ability to lay the right foundation; helping others over the mental and emotional stresses that comes with change. This is not done in large classrooms with PowerPoint presentations. It is done over coffee and a notepad; eyeball-to-eyeball and heart-to-heart. It requires social skills first.

So set aside the technical solutions for another day. Get out and talk with your trading partners. Tell them about your hopes and dreams; and find out about their desires. Don't get mired in the technical and don't try to map out all the answers: Tell them you are still looking for the right question. They will appreciate your honesty and the trust you build will do much to assure your future success. More importantly, they will want to do eBusiness with you.

A loving heart is the beginning of all knowledge

Thomas Carlyle (1795-1881)

It's All About Basics

We learn many simple skills of life in kindergarten. For some of us it is the first time we sit still for long periods of time. It may be the first time we are asked to be quiet and really listen to others. We take for granted the hot lunches that some children experience for the first time at kindergarten. It may be the first time a child has a teacher and a mentor.

Their parents send them into their classrooms with simple hopes and simple dreams. Many parents are filled with aspirations and expectations of their children. Their prayer is that their children will find encouragement here. They hope their hearts and minds will both be nourished.

For some of us it is the first time we pick up scissors or write on a chalkboard. With simple tools, like pencils and crayons, children enter a brave new world. Kindergarten is about simple work and simple play. It's all about basics.

Our life becomes more complex as we progress through grade school, high school, college, and into our professional careers. The business world tends to create all manner of new demands. For many of us, it means raising children and watching them cycle through grade school to college and the difficult choices they face, which mirror the difficult choices we faced at their age.

Looking back, we ask ourselves: *"When did life become so complicated?"*

B2B should really stand for "back to basics." The barrage of documents touting technology advances, multi-tier architectures, or open standards that I receive in my office is impressive. A virtual avalanche of information that is intended to sell me on the benefits of one vendor's solution over the next guy's solution. If only B2B were that simple. If all we had to do was buy the software and it magically just happened. But B2B is not about the technology being simple.

What are most frequently missing are the human aspects to go along with the technology. The marketing brochures don't focus on change management, if they touch on them at all. They slide right through the emotional wrangling people may go through. They slip past what makes B2B both hard and complex to implement.

I love the Gartner, Inc. "Hype Cycle."* It endeavors to place, on a time line, a picture of a technologies life from "spark" through hype to realization. Why it works so well is that it has nothing to do with technology. It is about human nature.

The "hype cycle" begins with a trigger-- some event or technology trigger that generates a spark in everyone's imagination. It goes next through a peak of inflated expectations, where the hype reaches its zenith. Often expanded by technology soothsayers, marketing, and the media, the fever grows unabated until reality pushes a nail through its puffed up veneer. "This is going to be a lot harder (cost more, be slower in coming) than we thought."

The over-inflated bubble pops and we go through the trough of disillusionment. Our unrealistic high meets an equally unrealistic low. Our disappointment shows on our faces until we step back and reassess what can be done during the slope of enlightenment. Yes, there is some kernel we can take away. Yes, there is something on which to build. Yes, we can make something work out of this disappointment. Finally we arrive at the plateau of productivity.

The cycle is equally applicable to dating, marriage, raising kids, and your career. It's not as much about technology as it is about human nature. It is about "us." It is about the part of us all that strives to find the "silver bullet." It is about the part of each of us that looks for the improbable: the new cancer treatment when hope has seemingly been lost and the home run with two outs in the bottom of the ninth to win the game. But we can endlessly search for the killer B2B application while missing wonderful opportunities.

And it is about our own laziness. The part of each of us that would like to find the new business breakthrough that will make us loads of money, fame, or the simple life. What we fail to grasp is that looking for the easy solution frequently makes things much harder for us. It leads us away from simple and away from basics.

Our attitude tends to be "if we build it, they will come," but we forget there is substantial preparation required ahead of time. Looking for the easy route distracts us from the pile of hard work setting just ahead of us. It is hard work making it look easy.

Some of my business associates have been sorely disappointed that their applications haven't achieved the business benefits that were detailed in their business cases. They spend their time revising their utilization or adoption projections or explaining to their bosses (or themselves) why it is going to take longer than they thought. They draw up revised implementation plans, which again will disappoint and create a new cycle of explanations to the boss (and themselves). Or they spend their time printing up brochures or preparing email blasts that sing of benefits, while missing the human nature aspects that really pave the way.

There should be spring training for B2B, where we work on fundamentals.

The good news is that there are only three things you have to do. The three things are better, faster, cheaper.

If you can do those three things simultaneously <u>and</u> if you can articulate these benefits <u>and</u> if your trading partner is sufficiently convinced to move with you, your plan is home free.

If you can do only two of those three, you may still be successful. But it will be far more difficult. You still have to articulate these benefits <u>and</u> convince your trading partner.

If you can do only one of those three, the road is even more difficult. It will be nearly impossible. You still have to articulate these benefits <u>and</u> convince your trading partner, but you can be easily sidetracked with questions of "offsets." "Sure, you can make it better, but will it cost more?"

The bad news is that there are three things you have to do. The three are better, faster, cheaper. You have to do all three simultaneously and substantially to guarantee you can get your plan accepted (and you still haven't even built anything yet).

Now the hard part: It's not about YOU! Remember our old friends better, faster, cheaper? That is better, faster, and cheaper <u>for your trading partner</u>, not for you. Once you have their side of the equation figured out, you need to translate that into the business benefits you will see on your side to determine whether you have a viable project.

It is easier to get your suppliers to do things than your customers. But, contrary to popular belief, it is still difficult to get your suppliers to do what you want. There are thousands of ways they can sidestep and delay.

First, you need to get into your trading partner's "heart and mind." It requires that you be so close to your customer that you can "project" yourself into their skin. You know them so well that you understand how they will react. You can move beneath what they say to what they feel. You will know what is behind what they say. You will know when what they say contradicts what they really want to say, and you will know why. You know when they are just "jockeying for position."

Then you can take it to your management to sell your project.

It's the business process... We overcomplicate on one hand and look for the easy way (no matter how complicated) on the other. We are far better off looking for simple approaches. Simple is not the same as easy. Simple starts with a realistic assessment of your current status and a hard look at the many opportunities that are before you.

Starting with the business process forces us "back to basics." It requires us to ask hard questions, "Why are we doing it this way?," "What is this intended to accomplish?," and "What are the fundamental steps the user will have to take?"

When we force ourselves to take a hard look at the business process, we put ourselves in our customer's shoes. In our minds, we stare at the computer screen in front of us as if we were the user and say, "Is this the best use my time? " and we are forced to ask ourselves, "Am I proud of what this design says about me?"

Looking at those opportunities through the filter of your trading partner's eyes brings you a realistic perspective of the landscape. The most fabulous solution that your trading partner will not or cannot implement is fruitless. Better to move on. Look to streamline the business process; eliminate valueless steps or processes. Look at the value of data throughout the information chain.

All this begins with surveying and documenting the business process from end to end. Everything drives from the business process. We need to continually remind ourselves, "It's the business process...." Each time we fall in love with the technology we have to remind ourselves, "It's the business process...." Each time it "clicks" that what we are suggesting may be too complicated, it is. Get back to basics by getting back to the business process.

We always seem to miss the fact that the business process is central to everything we do with B2B. The business process is how we measure and determine our probability of success. The business process is the only way we can communicate a vision to others. It is how we "sell" our programs to our management and our trading communities. We get excited about technologies and architectures, about new devices and hardware, while missing the most obvious factor for success-- "What can I really do with this?"

It is like deciding you are going to take a vacation and going out and buying a car. Then deciding that you are going to vacation in Tahiti! The purchase of car and the vacation no longer have anything to do with one another. The car isn't going to get you there. The car is not beneficial to the vacation. This is the same as when we design the B2B architecture and tools prior to defining our business process. Why do we tend to do that? It doesn't make sense when we look at it from a distance, but it usually is because the architecture has such a long purchase and development cycle. We need to start with a well-defined and crisply documented business requirement and business process flow.

How do we describe our business process? How do we explain and communicate all this? How do we document what needs to be built and what resources need to be "put together?"

I like to develop use cases to help understand how it will work. Use cases can be done in a variety of ways. You can buy software to create very elaborate documentation. While diagrams and charts and "swim lanes" have their place, for my money the most effective is a text based use case, supplemented by a few diagrams or high-level flow charts. For most applications, you can probably use tools you already have.

Use cases get down on paper what it is you are trying to build and accomplish. It details the business flow and captures issues and concerns. These are "living, breathing" documents that carry you from conception through development, testing, training, and implementation. These can run dozens or hundreds of pages. If they get to be too large, they should be broken into multiple smaller use cases that detail one small stream of the business process.

You may end up with many of these and one small, overarching use case that describes how all the "streams" come together. An analogy to an aerial photograph of a river delta gives us the best picture of this. Each river tributary has a use case, with a high-level use case that spans the entire delta.

A use case helps us keep focused on the business process.

Keeping it simple is hard work. Keeping things simple is probably the hardest work I do each day. It is easy to overly complicate things. It is easy to get lost on the road to success. It is easy to add one more bell or one more whistle. You may find your application overloaded. Your may find your plan bloated and in need of a diet. You can find what you have designed no longer meets the objectives. You can find you have to "back track" and eliminate some things from your design. This can be very difficult, especially if you have been "touting" some feature or function that has generated excitement. Going back and taking that off the drawing board can be painful and confusing to others.

There are other times you need to fight the impulse to take the easy approach because it is not the simple approach. Another global designer, Dorothy Erbacher, was working with me on what verbage to use to describe the status of a shipment in an order status application. The "native" API out of our backend application called a status "delivered" once data had been passed to our logistics application. Essentially, it was just notifying another application that the order could be filled and shipped. Internally we knew (and talked) in the language of the API. But "delivered" has a different meaning to the customer. It means the box is literally in their "hot little hands." We needed to search out the characteristics that best described the status of the shipment to the customer in the language that was most meaningful to them, and we needed to confirm that language with our customers. The easy way would be to use the applications description of the status. The simple way was to describe in language that best communicated reality to the customer. But the simple way was only simple in the end result; there was more work and more system logic necessary to make it simple for the user.

We have to continually "peel the onion," taking layer and layer of complexity away from our designs.

As a wise person pointed out, "The main thing is to keep the main thing the main thing." It applies to kindergarten and it applies to B2B. The main thing is staying with the basics. The business process is the "heart and soul" of B2B.

Keep it central. Keep it basic. Keep it simple.

"Genius is one percent inspiration and ninety-nine percent perspiration."

Thomas Alva Edison

* Hype Cycle is copyrighted and a registered trademark of Gartner, Inc.

Intuition

I still bear the crooked little finger on my left hand to remind me. I knew before I swung that it was a dumb idea. My intuition told me to stop, but some lessons have to be learned the painful way.

There was a boy in my neighborhood who really got on my nerves. He was always picking on me. He wasn't very big and I knew I could take him. One day we were playing baseball in my backyard. He pushed me just a bit too far. I had told him repeatedly that if he didn't "knock it off" I was going to "knock him off!" But he just kept after me.

I tried to ignore him, but he just continued to pester me. Something kept telling me to "just walk away." I knew this wasn't going to end well. I tried to get back to playing ball, but he nagged at me. The other guys tried to get both of us to stop and "just get back to the game."

I thought about how the guys would see me. If I backed down now I would be a chicken. If I slugged him I would be a hero, because I knew he bugged them, too. Yet, I also knew this would not be the end of it. I knew punishment was coming if I acted on my anger.

But I couldn't stop myself. I couldn't ignore him. I was fuming. He pushed and pushed. I just knew my mom was going to kill me if I slugged him. I could hear the speech coming, "What got into you?" I could feel the disappointment she would express. I could hear her curt, sharp remarks already. My intuition told me to stop; my anger told me to kill!

The next time he pushed is when I snapped. I threw down my bat and charged. Where he had been standing, I could see I had him cornered. I had seen a lot of westerns on TV and so I pretty well knew how to do this. Man-to-man combat. No big deal. Standing there slugging it out. I knew I could whip him.

What I didn't figure on is that he would duck. I also didn't remember that there was a redwood fence immediately behind his head. Funny, I had lived there my whole life; you would think I would remember the small detail of the redwood fence when I followed up the right jab with that ill-fated left hook!

I endured the pain and didn't even let my mom look at it. I hid the fact that I had hurt myself. It hurt far into the night. The guys wouldn't tell on me, so I thought I was home clear. I thought the pain in my hand was lesson enough.

Other than him ducking and the redwood fence, the other thing I hadn't figured on was him telling the principal...until the vice-principal called me out of class the following morning.

eBusiness is more about intuition that anything else I have experienced in my business career. Messages are coming at us from all directions. Frequently these messages conflict with one another. The pace of development is astonishing. Nothing ever seems to be on a straight route. You finally see a technology that will solve an age-old problem and you think you are all set! Until you realize it causes two other problems. Then you go after those issues. And so B2B goes.

Nothing is ever straightforward and direct. Either the technology isn't ready or the business partners aren't ready. Standards that sound so good fall short for unexpected reasons. Half the battle is figuring out what will not work and crossing that off the list of potential solutions. Most times you just have to trust your gut.

People always say, "Give the customer what they want." I have yet to hear what the customer really wants when I first talk to them about it. Generally, it takes a few times to get beyond the short-term issues. It also takes a period of developing trust. That requires commitment and consistent behavior from your whole organization. So if you think you are going to just waltz into a customer's location and find out what they want, think again. Plan for it that way. Accept the alternate route to success; step back to get their short-term objectives (which may have nothing to do with eBusiness) out of the way, to get to the long-term objectives.

Be leery of anyone who wants to do eBusiness with you, but cannot articulate crisp and specific objectives. If someone says they "want to (or worse yet, must) save money", run away. If someone says "we can each save 10% on our costs by doing step a, b and c;" listen.

In the day-to-day activities of the work world, we rarely have time to sit back and think about what we want from our suppliers and customers. We take even less time delving into what our customers want and need.

I worked in a three-tier supply chain business (manufacturer to distributor to user) where prices were being negotiated between the manufacturer and user, but the distributor needed to manage the distribution and payment cycles. It was a pretty typical three-tier supply chain arrangement and not a pretty picture for knowing what the customer wants. After all, who is the customer? The one who buys? The one who influences the purchase? What about when the distributor and user don't agree? Not always clear.

When we talked to the distributor about his problems, he came up with elaborate solutions that would have been difficult to manage. We could have built expensive and complex eBusiness mechanisms to improve the communications and cycle-time. If we had listened to these customers' initial needs, we would have.

But delving deeper into the problem gave us an opportunity to look at it differently. It allowed us to reengineer the business process, so that when we executed the eBusiness solution that complemented the process, it was simple, straightforward, and less costly. But we had to trust our gut in order to propose that solution. We had to look beyond today's issues and problems and change our paradigm.

Ignorance is not bliss; ignorance is ignorance. "No information" is never the preferred approach. We have such bad supply chain processes in one business that it is nearly impossible to quote a delivery date for a product that is even remotely accurate.

As a result, the business has their employees quote "six months" when asked when something will be delivered. When pressed they will work to get a more accurate date, which is more likely to be two or three months out. The thought is if we give the customer a date that is always "far out" (bad information), but deliver to a better date (good reality), that will satisfy the customer.

In fact, perception is reality. The business failed to recognize three things: 1) requiring the customer to come back to get information they needed was a major irritant, 2) customers expect that you know "sometime" in order to run your business and, therefore, we must have been hoarding information for some reason, and 3) the customer already knew we have lousy supply chain processes. For us, it is just information, but they lived our supply chain problems.

I know what you are thinking, "I can't give information that he can use to hang me!" Wrong attitude. Instead, look at it this way, "You deserve to be hung! Now what are you going to do about it?"

Don't get trapped into thinking you need to fix the supply chain before you can or have to fix the information chain. Use the information chain, internally and externally, as your report card for improving the process. They go hand-in-hand. You can't wait.

Trading partners dissatisfied with the information they receive? You have found an ideal place to apply eBusiness.

Watch for "human lubricant." Also known as "sneakerware" or "throwing bodies" at a problem. This is when the flow of information or products requires "extra people" to maintain, manage, or smooth the business process. We tend to see it everywhere. It may be where we have set up a pilot process and don't want to change the back office applications to support it. Or where the business has outpaced the information systems and so we setup "one off" business processes to manage the disparity.

In effect, we "smooth" the rough spots by lubricating the process with people-- "holding hands", monitoring, expediting the activities, doing "whatever it takes" to make the process work with minimal friction for the customer.

We had all our systems geared to a multiple level warehousing operation. We would manufacture items and then place them in warehouses around the country where they could be consolidated with many other items for efficient delivery to many customers. It was slow and expensive, but worked reasonably well for many years. Until we needed to move product from the manufacturing plant directly to customers using full truckload deliveries.

The business processes and systems weren't structured to support those processes, so we added people to "align" the real product flow to the information flow. But filling the gap was expensive.

The hard part is that you need to look for these things at both your site and your trading partner's site. We typically have enough problems without going outside our four walls to find more!

Throwing bodies at your business problems? You have found an ideal place to apply eBusiness.

eBusiness drives a different business case. There is all manor of bad information out there. There are many poor ways at looking at the data. There are many "self preservation" biases we hear. You need to get beyond all of that when your instinct tells you.

Here are the truths concerning eBusiness business cases:

- ❏ There are only two types: bad and lucky.

- ❏ Figures lie and liars figure.

- ❏ There are far too many unknowns to do a thorough business case.

- ❏ Like sands through an hourglass, your competitive advantage is slipping away.

- ❏ When you get right down to it, "You have to trust your gut."

If eBusiness were easy, management wouldn't need us. If you think you can wait until the technology "sorts itself out," think again. If you think you can wait until the entire "math equation" makes sense, think again.

In some instances you need to resist the impulse to move forward. In the same way, I needed to resist the impulse to throw a punch; there can be unconsidered or unseen consequences in our acts. But you also can't afford to wait too long. You can get killed in going too slowly as in going too fast. In the end, you have to trust your instinct to tell you when the time is right. And when it is, act decisively.

"Damn the torpedoes! Full speed ahead!"

David G. Farragut, Battle of Mobile Bay, August 5, 1864

Do What You Do Well

I was always good at drawing. But I couldn't draw the things my friend next door, Gary Oien, could draw. Or, maybe, I just didn't want to draw what he liked to draw. He liked to draw dinosaurs in fierce battles. His drawings would be without backgrounds and would intensely portray the combatants biting, clawing, and snapping. They were immense in both size and furiousity. The blood flowed all across the pages.

My drawings were mostly of landscapes. They would show good proportions, perspective, and shadows. I didn't do as well showing action scenes. I did well drawing people, as long as they weren't in motion. In Sunday school class, we were told to draw a picture of our fathers for Father's Day. I don't know why my mother was so embarrassed; I drew him in an anatomically correct fashion!

It is hard to tell whether I didn't draw dinosaurs well because I couldn't or didn't like to draw them. I would try, but it just didn't feel right. It just wasn't fun. Eventually both Gary and I would sit at the kitchen table and draw what we liked and what we did well. I didn't even try to draw dinosaurs any more and Gary didn't try to draw landscapes. Yet we could both enjoy drawing together, side-by-side, and both drawing well based on our interests.

Miss Waters encouraged all the kids in kindergarten to draw. She taught us some simple skills and provided opportunities for us to try new things in art. My mother also encouraged me to draw. She was pleased by what I did and encouraged me to show my drawing to others. In later years, she helped me obtain art supplies and expanded my horizon to learn to paint. As with most things in life, you enjoy them more if you do them well.

As companies we should seek out those B2B projects that we can do well. That is not to say we shouldn't try new things. But it is to say, just like people, companies have personalities. Technologies and projects that run counter to those personalities aren't as likely to be successful. They certainly aren't the most fun on which to work.

As an individual, you should consider passing on projects that don't interest you or that you don't feel you do as well as others. It is better to know yourself and excel at projects that fit your skills and interest than in trying to be "all things to all people." Be selective and search for projects that will provide the best returns within the confines of your interests. Finding these "matches" will insure the highest probability of personal success.

Look for "technology matches." There are two aspects of technology match that you need to consider.

The first question you should be asking is, "What is a good technology match for my trading partners?"

There is a difference between when trading partners say they are ready and when they are actually ready. I have had it occur a number of times when customers have come to us to access our readiness for a technology. Sometimes we have done very detailed and elaborate evaluations and usually we found application for the technology. Sometimes we found things that didn't meet our needs "somewhere" in the company, but not very often. After a cursory look at a technology, I finally wised up and began saying, "When you are ready, we will be ready!"

There are times trading partners need to be educated, such as blowing away the myths about EDI or XML. There are other times they need both education and socialization, such as with bar code processing and hand held scanners or Voice over Internet Protocol (VoIP).

There are times when the socialization hasn't caught up, such as with public exchanges. Until the risks (or apparent risks) are moderated, the mating dances will continue.

So what should you look for in a technology? Start with the lowest common denominator and work your way up the technology complexity ladder. What technology can be proliferated throughout your trading community? Don't assume anything. Access the ability of your trading partner. You may be shocked at what some company's policies and practices may prevent you from doing. Don't ask the business people; ask the IS people.

The second question is, "What is a good technology match for me?" This is where we need to set our egos aside and go through a similar exercise in asking the same question about a technology match for our trading partners. Having gone through the questions for our trading partners allows us the ability to assess ourselves.

Companies put together their technologies in a somewhat haphazard way. It comes with "fits and starts." Only when pressure has built up do we get beyond studying something -- sometimes to death. Normally there is external pressure that drives our eBusiness solutions and we are highly influenced by exactly what the trading partner is pressing us to implement.

Other times we build a technology, based on our own interests. But when we select that technology we preclude investment in parallel technologies that may be an equally good or better fit.

After you have considered those two questions, what looks like a good fit? Only when your technology preference and ability is the same as your trading partners' technology preference and ability do you have a technology match. This "superset" of technologies is the best possible match. That is what you both can and will do well.

If you want to be a leader in B2B, you need to be willing to make the investment in technologies, long before your customers and suppliers are ready. Count on some of these failing. Count of some of these being great dreams, but ultimately poor fits. You will waste money in the short term, but will be well prepared when that sweet "superset" of technologies shows up on the horizon.

Look for "skill fit." Just like Gary and me with drawing, each of us had different skills. We brought to the kitchen table different perspectives on beauty, power, and motion. We both excelled in the type of art that interested us.

Sometimes we excel at things we don't enjoy very much. I do a pretty good job at designing EDI transactions. I can see the data coming out of one application and into another. I can visualize the data requirements and the business process flows at both companies. I can determine the value (or lack of value) of the information to both parties. Frankly, I am good at it. That doesn't mean I enjoy it as much as I once did. After you have designed hundreds of EDI transactions, it becomes pretty routine. But there still are times when my expertise comes into play. There are times when I can add value that nobody around me has the expertise or background to provide.

There are also times when the skill from one area can be transferred to a new area. I was involved with a billing company on a project where they had built a series of file transfers to supplement their web-based application. It certainly wouldn't have been the way I would have designed the process, however, they were already in production with a number of large customers. Rather than "rocking the boat" and demanding a whole new set of functions, we incorporated what they had in place with our capability. We helped them understand the issues and constraints of their application. That was based on knowledge of the value (and limitations) that EDI brought to the table for large file transfer type processes.

You want to excel at things you enjoy most. It makes work fun. But you also want to make sure that you are nurturing the right future skills at your company. If you don't, you limit the capability that can be created or you make it far more expensive to achieve.

Most of the skills needed are built upon the base of previous technologies. A great deal can be learned about the strengths and weaknesses of XML, for example, by studying the security issues you have faced in the past from transmitting data around your companies. Unfortunately, once problems are "conquered" we tend to forget or take for granted what we have learned.

Look for "personality fit." Both companies and individuals have personalities. Kodak has been a leader in wireless applications in manufacturing and distribution. But we don't seem to have the "personality" to take some of those activities outside our walls.

If your bent is operational excellence, use B2B for operational excellence. If you are focused on customer intimacy, use B2B to further that goal if and when your customer heads in that direction. If your company is focused on product leadership, embed them with eBusiness applications and technologies that further your leadership. Stay narrowly focused on your corporate mission.

I most enjoy working on the transactional side of B2B, but the field is ripe for implementing high quality content and information features. Personally, much of it bores me. I could do it. But I would probably never excel at it. It is the space I want to avoid.

Fortunately, there are plenty of activities in the B2B space at most companies. Pick those that are right for you.

Do what you do well. Focus on that in which you excel. Let your brilliance shine in the places you want to shine. Don't be different for the sake of show. Don't be contrary to yourself. Doing well in B2B starts with knowing yourself--as companies and as people.

"If there is anything that a man can do well, I say let him do it. Give him a chance."

Abraham Lincoln

Wonder

Many days, especially during spring, we would walk home after school. It wasn't far and there were many diversions on our path. We would play catch or throw rocks as we crossed the schoolyard to leave by the rear gate. We would play marbles on the hardpan areas where many shoes had first erased the grass, than prevented the replacement seeds from sprouting. Or we would take a swing at an imaginary baseball and run around the bases to slide into third base before the imaginary tag. A triple!

There was a small creek near school. Actually we just called it a creek; it wasn't a creek at all. It was a small, fenced off storm drain that contained a small amount of water year round (probably just sprinkler runoff) and was only full immediately following a big rain.

The concrete near the drain was slimy with strings of green moss. Long, dark "feelers" of moss swayed in the trickle of water, holding on tight to the concrete to keep from being washed away.

Usually there wasn't much to see in the creek. One of my friends had gone down there one weekend with his father to capture pollywogs. They took mason jars and scooped up some of the gray creatures. The pollywogs were always in motion, wiggling, fighting against the current. They brought them home and Jon kept them out in his garage. His mom wouldn't think of having them in the house. Each day we would dump a little turtle food in the jars, though I don't remember ever seeing them actually eat.

We would watch them for a few minutes every day to see what was new and different. I couldn't believe what Jon was telling me-- that these squiggly little things were going to get fat and grow legs. Initially they were only about a quarter inch long. In a short time they had doubled in both length and width. His dad would tell him what we could expect to see next and he would relay the stories on to us. At first we didn't really believe him. It was just too strange to believe. But we watched as each step unfolded as his dad had foretold. Soon we were able to notice stubs of legs beginning to appear. Then they became full-formed legs with flippers.

Not long afterward, we had an explosion of frogs in the neighborhood.

In is wonderful to see the unexpected in eBusiness. I remember once debating the "wisdom" of telling our distributors when we projected their deliveries of materials to arrive. We had a fair amount of variability in our supply chain. Our age old practice had been to tell customers to expect the delivers in seven-to-ten days. We thought that was pretty good; it seemed to cover the bases-- over ninety-nine percent of our situations. About the only time we took longer than two weeks was for "make to order" items or real screw-ups. We were "fat, dumb, and happy" that this was the best we could do and distributors were happy with the "seven-to-ten day" response. Or so we thought.

It was interesting to talk to these distributors to see what seven-to-ten days meant to them. We were surprised by their answer--no, shocked. Almost every one of them told us it meant seventeen calendar days. That blew us away!

But their logic made a great deal of sense once we viewed it through their eyes. It turned out they were taking a worse case scenario (of ten days), interpreting that as working days (which adds on weekends), then adding three days of in-transit time for seventeen calendar days. Since that was such a long time out and since there was a good deal of variability, they wouldn't even plan deliveries to their customers against the information. Instead, they would wait until the materials were delivered to schedule those deliveries! To their customers they would quote the same lead-time we did and if that was not satisfactory, they would typically inventory stock for their customers.

In hindsight, it is now amazing that we thought we could get away with it!

When we evaluated our actual deliveries from end-to-end, we found that 80% of them were hitting on the eighth day (plus or minus one day) after ordering. We believed we didn't have a very good story to tell our pilot customers. In fact, just the opposite was true. Our distributors were ecstatic.

They recognized that they could "plan" based on the small delivery date range variability. Even though they had to make some minor adjustments based on the twenty percent of the time we did not make the estimate, this was a great improvement over their earlier experience. Now they could tell their customers eight days instead of seventeen days.

Our evaluations previously had shown that we were "consistent, but slow" in making deliveries. Now they saw us as having made aggressive improvements in our supply chain and that we had dramatically improved the cycle time! Now they viewed us as "consistent, fast, and willing to take bold actions to improve supply."

All the work in collecting the data further enabled us to make changes to the supply chain. These were "substitutive" changes, but our customers viewed this as sustained, continuous improvement. They believed that improvement was becoming a way of life for us.

Poor information led to poor behaviors on our part, which led to poor information on our customers' part. The real impact was on the consumers. Improved information flow improved the relationship as well as the perceived and real supply chain.

We have to look beyond what customers are telling us. It takes a special kind of listening to customers to be extremely effective. Customers will start talking about today's situation and work their way forward. But they will do so in "building block" fashion. Only when you have taken in, understood, and responded to the issues of today will they be readily willing to move forward with you. They need to see results. Results build confidence. Repeated satisfactory responses to issues builds trust. Once you have trust, they are willing to move forward with you into the future.

The operative word in the previous sentence is "willing." You can force change on customers and inherit the whirlwind. At best, you can force change on customers and deal with continual resistance. The alternative is to develop the foundation--the building blocks, that helps them willingly move forward into the future with you. If you do the latter, the transition is emotionally and mentally easier. You don't end up having to fight two fires at one time--one to proceed with your project and another to keep distractions bounded.

Customers are willing to dream with you. But there is an investment on their part that they have to be willing to make. They have to see that their investment will pay a future dividend, in some form--faster, better, cheaper. The likelihood that the dividend can be realized is directly portioned to the confidence that customers have that you will do "your part." That is where your history plays a vital role.

Once they can dream with you, expect it to take a great deal of effort to drill down to enable process improvement. They will continually view issues in terms of today's behavior. You have to help them, and yourself, see how the world can be different. Help see what can be thrown out. Help see how business can be dramatically different. Together you can dream. Together you can wonder how to build a better future.

We have to expect the unexpected. Just as when I watched pollywogs turn into frogs, we have to expect the unexpected. There have been times I have looked back and said to myself, "Why didn't I see that it would happen that way?"

B2B developments can lead to opportunities that cannot be foretold. Sometimes what you develop gets whispered from customer to customer. The opportunities come back to us when we least expect them.

Once I was asked to make a presentation at a business meeting of all the US dealers in one channel. It was followed by a dinner to which I hadn't been invited. That changed when some accolades rolled in at the end of the presentation, which were echoed by some others. The acknowledgment was gratifying, but it didn't influence my future success. Success started by being "set up" in front of other dealers with whom I hadn't worked before. Those who had waited for others to pioneer knew that they could come to me for help. I couldn't have paid for that kind of advertising.

Other times our applications "sprout legs." They not only go places and are used in ways that we don't anticipate, but sometimes they are contrary to what we design. We built a B2B order entry, order status, and carrier tracking application for customer usage. We were attempting to make it easy to use and highly intuitive. We also built in features that made it better for our employees. It described things in better ways and linked directly to carriers' web sites. We had built it with the customer in mind. But our employees found great value in it as well. They clamored for access.

Go after a different paradigm. Albert Einstein said, "The important thing is not to stop questioning." We need to remain unsatisfied with what we have done. We need to look beyond what we have accomplished to determine how we can make things better. That means being willing to throw things out and begin again.

Those of us who have been in the B2B space for a long time have seen the changes in a different light. We watched B2B solutions (proprietary file transfer, EDI, web-based, and XML) enter the landscape. Most of the trade literature has viewed each new technology with one thought: "Out with the old and in with the new." But the wonder of it all has not been technology displacement (which hasn't occurred much), but how one stage of the business process has built upon the previous.

If anything, the technology has taken us a step backward. Many of the proponents of both web- and XML-based solutions have stumbled. They didn't understand the need to look backward to see what had been learned before it earlier eCommerce efforts. They took for granted the failures and trials of the past. They have stumbled on many of the same issues that had been conquered sometimes a quarter of a century before.

We need to question everything--the past as well as the future.

Wonder frees us to think beyond today's paradigms. Wonder allows us to dream with our customer and suppliers of a better tomorrow. Wonder allows us to conjure B2B solutions that are unimaginable today.

"Wisdom begins in wonder."

Socrates

Trust

The memory I had of nurses when I was in kindergarden was painful. I was either sick when I saw one or was going to get a shot. There were no "in-between" visits, no social calls.

I remember once having a childhood physical and the doctor ordered a shot. The nurse stretched down my undershorts to expose my hip. Then I felt immense pain. But it didn't take long before it stopped, because the nurse had stopped trying to push in the needle. She explained to me that I was tightening up my butt so much, she couldn't get the needle in! We were probably going to be there all day unless I relaxed.

She told me to look at the pictures on the wall. She told me it wouldn't hurt. She was right; looking at the pictures didn't hurt. She assured me she would let me know when she was going to try to give me the shot again. So I stood there, bent over with my butt hanging out for what seemed like eternity. I carefully studied the handful of old pictures on the wall of the examination room.

Then, unannounced, she came back and nailed me. That lying, stealth nurse. She didn't tell me it was coming, like she had promised. She hadn't knocked on the door. She must have "tip toed" in while I was concentrating on the pictures. While it got the immediate job done, it did have a lasting impression on me.

So when, a few weeks later, I was sent to see the school nurse, I didn't quite know what to expect. But I certainly wasn't thrilled. She didn't seem to be all that different. She wore the same uniform and the same hat. She immediately recognized my apprehension. She told me it wouldn't hurt. Yeah, I'd heard that one before. She explained the test she was going to give me. She gave it to me "step-by-step." It was a hearing test and I was to wear heavy, black earphones and tell her when I heard small beeps and in which ear I heard them. She took the time to explain the equipment she was going to use and how the test worked.

She told me that if I didn't pass the test, they would make sure I sat closer to the teacher and she would give me special attention. She also told me that if I didn't pass the test, I would need to see some doctors. I asked her if that would hurt and she told me she didn't know. She was honest with me. Then she said, "This is just a test we are giving every kindergartener. I don't expect any of you to fail."

"Okay, " I said. We proceeded with the test.

A lifetime of trust can disappear with the wrong step. Trust is about keeping first things first. It is about reassuring people of the steps that need to be followed and why--even the steps that may be painful or difficult.

It is amplified with B2B. The crash of the "dot-coms" should be a lesson in trust to all of us. We trusted others and optimism, when we should have been looking at fundamentals. When companies were bleeding resources profusely, we should have questioned their ability to stand on their own. In fact, speculators propped them up and we didn't want to see that as a red flag. They weren't realizing profit on the immediate horizon, while telling us of their glorious business model that would provide spectacular returns in the not-too-distant future. We still didn't see the red flags.

They confused customer payment with investment capital. They thought these monies coming in to their companies were the same thing, when they should have been writing them down on opposing sides of the ledger. And we bought it: Shame on us.

They asked us to trust them, and they hadn't earned our trust. We pay for our mistakes. They'd best not try that again.

The feeling of trust (or mistrust) is transferable. We all have been in the situation where a colleague has promised something to a customer and never delivered. Then when we meet the customer, we are expected to not only explain the other person's behavior, but also "pick up the pieces."

This happens all too frequently in business. We are all busy. We all get preoccupied. When we are with the customer, we write actions down on our "to do list" or place 3M Post-its™ all over the edge of our computer screens. Those "notes" come with the good intentions of following up on that product return that should have been credited by now, or creating that special extract, or setting up that "uncomfortable" meeting with the management team.

We have left the customer with the impression that we would follow through on something. We view it as just another task of uncertain importance; they view it as a commitment.

So when the note falls off the computer screen and we cannot read our writing any longer, or it gets passed over to the IS department and placed on the stack of a zillion other things to get to "some day," or gets tossed out in the despair of ever getting caught up, we have actually betrayed a trust.

I wish I could count the number of times I have walked into a customer site to explain a new B2B feature and was handed a task like this, which I consider outside of "my realm."

Whether you want it or not-- "Tag, you're it!"

It has now become your job to get it done and to satisfy the customer. It is your job to follow through to completion. This is not just calling Bob to see if he has done something; this is calling Bob, facilitating the completion, and going over Bob's head if necessary. Doing "whatever it takes" and then closing the loop with the customer.

Trust is transferable. Mistrust is transferable. Our trading partners believe we come out of the same training school (and to some degree we do). They believe it is not just Bob who has failed; it is your whole company that has failed. If Bob can't get it done, why should Duane be able to get it done?

Trust can be spent, either intentionally or unintentionally. Others can spend it in your company on your behalf, such as your boss. If you make a commitment to attend a function or make a speech and your boss takes away money for the travel budget, for example, he has jeopardized your relationship. He has spent "trust" on your behalf. For a while you can no longer be trusted to make certain commitments. You now may need to qualify your commitments. You now have baggage to take on your journey with trading partners. That can be a heavy load.

With B2B we bring a new agenda to the table, but we also bring with it our track record as a company and as individuals. We are in the daily battle of proving ourselves.

Trust is not a "sometime" thing. We need to demonstrate consistency in our B2B dealings. When trust is lost, we need to understand what caused it to be lost. We need to face the failure in a forthright fashion and rectify the situation, where possible. This means getting down to the root cause and taking corrective action to permanently monitor and prevent its repeated occurrence.

You need to think of B2B as not only a better way of handling transactions, but also establishing a better relationship with your trading partners. Maybe you cannot (or even should not) deal with how things have been handled in the past. But you certainly have control and responsibility over the future.

A large part of reestablishing or, for that matter, establishing trust is communication. We have to tell people what is going to happen. We have to reassure people (in and out of our organizations) of the steps that need to be followed. We need to be clear about the uncertainties we have and how we may be mitigating risk. We need to facilitate communication (in multiple directions) to the point of over communication.

Trust must be demonstrated. Praise others for their trustworthiness. Acknowledge it when you observe it in others. But be cautious about expounding your own trustworthiness. Why? Trustworthiness is a perceived value. What is important is how others judge us, not how we judge ourselves. A simple misunderstanding can have long-term impacts. It can be perceived as a failure of trust when it really should not be. Regardless of whether or not it is a failure of trust, the resolution is the same--communication, driving down to the root cause, resolution, restoration, and reconciliation.

Trust is something that has to be nurtured. In our busy lives we tend to get distracted. We put off making that phone call or writing that note to the customer. Once it is put off, it becomes increasingly difficult to get it back to the top of the priority list.

I used to set aside one day every other week to call customers. I had over 80 customers with whom I was implementing an EDI solution. I wanted to communicate: encourage, check status, cajole, thank, or just say "hi." It was brutal.

There were lots of returned calls and messages. There was lots of catching people at the wrong time. Plus a good deal of "follow-up" work slithered back onto my plate. But two weeks later, come "hell or high water," they received another call from me.

It got easier for me and for my customers over time. They probably didn't know I was calling the whole market, but they did know I was going to be persistent with them. They knew I wasn't going to take up their valuable time (but they probably didn't know why-- that I had 79 other calls to make). They learned I couldn't escape completing all those follow-up activities that resulted from earlier calls. They learned they could not either. They learned to trust me. Not just that I would communicate with them again soon, but that I would report my lack of progress, my confusions and my failures as well. They learned to trust that I was a man of my word, and when I had let them down once, they knew I would redouble my efforts to get it right the second time. It is far easier to nurture a relationship than to reestablish one. But it needs and deserves our full attention. This is the hard work behind B2B.

In B2B, we need to consider trust a "high calling." Most of us never intentionally try to be untrustworthy. It isn't our nature or our character. We like a view of ourselves as people upon whom others can depend.

We have a view of the business world where trust is only important some of the time. It is only important when it serves a specific purpose. In B2B, however, trust is important all the time. By nature, B2B engages other companies. We rely on other companies for our success. We cannot do it alone.

We also live in a time when technology options abound. These two factors, taken together, help us understand that we need to mutually agree upon our path forward, timing, and resources. We need to implement with both the tools and the people with whom we are comfortable. One company can take the lead, but others need to be in full agreement.

Sometimes there need to be incentives to get others to invest. But at the foundation there needs to be agreement and commitment to do the work together. We might be able to get others to do their part once by threat or sheer force, but that fails over time. Certainly they would not seek us out the next time, if an interesting business opportunity came along.

Real trust, however, prevails. When we have successfully taken others through a project, when we have demonstrated commitment and built trust, then the next time we propose a project, everything goes much easier and faster.

Trust is built. Trust is earned. There is no easy path, no magic formula. Not only is it hard work, it has to be consistently applied. We have to make it a top priority.

Trust dies but mistrust blossoms.

Sophocles (497-405 B.C.)

Evaluating Others' Skills

Karen Thomas had flowing dark brown hair-- always with ribbons or bows. She was petite and graceful. Her eyes were coal black. I will never forget her wonderful smile. Both her smile and Karen were sweet and kind. Her hearing problem made her seem to concentrate more on her school activities. She was an only child, from a broken marriage.

But she couldn't play kickball. I think you had to have the influence of a brother or father to play kickball well. It is essential to have a basic understanding of baseball to know how to move around the bases. You have to move beyond the fear of pain or injury to really kick the ball with any gusto. These are all things that Karen could have developed if she had someone to help her along.

When we would choose up sides for kickball, she was typically one of the last ones chosen. When it was her turn to kick, the pitcher would roll the ball to her and she would give it her typical kick. It would hardly make it back to the pitcher. Automatic out. In the field, we would put her into right field. She was good at running down the ball, but didn't have the muscle to get it back into the infield.

I would have more success choosing Bonnie Byers, Carol Cook, or Earleen Fountain. When it came to kickball, you had to choose who would help you win.

It took me until 6thgrade to finally, fully appreciate Karen's finer qualities!

It is the same in eBusiness; you have to choose wisely the ones with whom to play. I laugh at the magazine advertisements that proclaim how much money they have saved with "their solution." They don't show the pain and suffering it has taken to get there. They haven't shown the hidden, ugly side of the implementation. All smiles and no sweat and toil. The haven't advertised the untold costs in time, money, and relationships. The advertisements don't tell the real tale. I would like to be able to look behind the scenes of those advertisements to see how much more could have been accomplished. Usually, that tells a far more interesting story. I have observed businesses force their suppliers into solutions, only to see additional costs get passed back (money, service levels, quality) that don't show up in the advertisements. I have seen high levels of production support activities going on behind the scenes as we apply "sneakerware, baling wire, and bandages" to keep things moving along. I have seen initiatives that have shown so much promise "die on the vine" based on sheer resistance.

At one company I worked with, we had 25% penetration in bringing suppliers on board using EDI. We would organize annual "conferences" (normally in the middle of winter in Rochester, New York) to bring the "uninitiated" back to talk through what they needed to do to get ready. The reward for doing EDI with us would be to get to miss out on the annual pilgrimage.

Business readiness is a huge issue. We would show our PowerPoints with all the diagrams of cost savings they could expect. We would line up software vendors who could help them implement. We would threaten, plead, and cajole. We would pull in our senior managers to discuss why this was important. Everything the book said to do. And next year, we would see the same familiar faces.

We would latch onto a few fish every year, but we never really got down to basics. That's hard work. This is a daunting task across thousands of vendors, to say the least. Instead, we would handle this in mass audiences in auditoriums. It wasn't personal. It wasn't sufficiently directed. What we needed to be doing was jointly accessing the potential trading partners' capabilities and identifying plans to get ready. We needed to identify how we would share the benefits, especially as they related to their business. We needed to know enough about their businesses to understand their issues (and vice versa). We needed to work through every aspect of our implementation together.

It isn't enough to tell the supplier "it is a lower cost business model" or "you are going to have to absorb the additional costs." These aren't stupid people. They didn't just fall off the turnip truck. They must be smart or they wouldn't be in business long. They wouldn't have made it through the gauntlet to become one of our prized suppliers. They know how to give with one hand while taking with the other. They know what is measurable and what is not. They know what is sustainable and what isn't. They do a great job looking into our eyes and accessing whether we will stand by what we threaten to do.

Access your trading partners' business readiness. There is a different criterion that needs to be applied for your trading partners than you may have previously applied. Accessing their technical readiness is likely checking their muscles to see if they have the "physical" abilities for eBusiness. Whether they have the coordination and technical wherewithal to pull B2B off.

But accessing their business readiness is a totally different issue. It is in knowing if their "heart and mind" are in it as well. It is whether their business mission and vision is aligned and supported by their eBusiness strategies and tactics. Essentially, it runs down two alternative paths-- either risk or reward.

Businesses come to B2B because they have recognized a competitive threat. They hear from their customers that their competitor is doing "such and such" and they believe it is essential they respond.

They believe their customers have mandated (or will mandate) a certain course of action and they have no other option. They believe they will either lose their preferred vendor status, or the business entirely, if they do not implement as they have been told.

Or they recognize some advantage they can apply. They see some opportunity in getting closer to their customer, to take cost out of the business process, or to extend some product or service they offer.

The worst scenario is when they try to see it both ways. Be cautious when you hear, "Our customer is making us do this, besides there are some opportunities here..." This is a set up for disaster.

To think that way is to be position yourself to do neither. You will not know when to step on the brake and when to step on the gas. You will not have the conviction to turn the keys of the car over to the racecar driver. You will spend your time debating whether what you are doing is meeting the customer need with any particular activity or furthering your competitive position.

If you don't know why you are doing B2B, you cannot be highly successful with B2B. Period. Business units cannot possibly align their eBusiness strategies and tactics with their business goals unless they have can see 1) alignment between the two and 2) their future state. Corporate strategies are generally conflicting and present an excessively broad vision and mission statement to apply in an exacting fashion to business units. There are some notable exceptions, but not enough to worry about.

About every five years, General Electric initiates a corporate strategy such as Quality, Electronic Commerce, or Workout™. These are sufficiently broad so that they can be adapted and molded to their specific business unit requirement. These are also sufficiently rare so that they are not viewed as the "program of the year," to be ignored sufficiently long that they "die away," as takes place at so many companies.

By nature, the BU strategies are where the rubber meets the road. It is where the acid test is applied to our business strategies.

Know what's in it for them. Until your trading partners have defined their mission and vision, you really cannot help them meet their eBusiness goals. Their goals will, by definition, be short term and misdirected.

Does this mean they cannot do B2B? No. But it does mean their B2B initiatives will likely be haphazard, disconnected, and uncoordinated. We have a retail customer who came to us in four months with three different proposals for B2B on three different platforms. Two of those solutions were web-based order management applications on separate platforms--one for direct materials and one for indirect materials. When we pointed out the disparity to their senior management, they thanked us and walked away to figure out where they were headed.

Sometimes businesses will know that they want to do something with you, but aren't quite sure what that is. It may be that you can get them to adopt your B2B initiative. On the surface, this may seem fine-- even the easy route. However, you still want to work through with them the value that they will see from doing your initiative. Why? So that when you are "down to the wire" on implementation, when the effort has gotten very hard, they will not back away at the last minute.

How, then, should we respond? Should you only do B2B with trading partners who have strategies and know where they are going? If the answer to that were yes, nobody would ever get anywhere!

You should partner with those who are further along in their thinking and planning, while you nurture those who are not as far along.

Work primarily with those who are 1) already aligned with where you want to go or 2) are willing to look into aligning with your strategy.

That doesn't mean to forget those who are not perfectly aligned with you. You still want to see if you can come together and do a bit of "horse trading."

You will need to place different emphasis on your program to the different sets of trading partners. With those that are ready, begin to solidify plans and building relationships. For those that are further behind, begin to educate and help them move forward. Think of these as becoming a stream of implementation.

All of this requires that you evaluate your trading partners skills and abilities. It requires that you take the additional step to access their eBusiness strategy and readiness.

A company with an eBusiness strategy can get any technical misalignment straightened away very quickly. But a technically savvy company cannot get an eBusiness strategy put in place quickly. One readiness speaks of leadership, the other does not.

Choose wisely. Choose based on business readiness first.

"Do what you can, with what you have, where you are."

Theodore Roosevelt

Letting Others Go First

Do you remember when you were dismissed for recess? At Mulberry Elementary School, we would all race to the swing sets. The swing sets were straight out from the doors, next to the end of the pavement. There was other playground equipment, such as "jungle gyms" and the sandboxes, but nothing quite like those swing sets.

We had a swing set at home, but it wasn't nearly as tall as these swings. The one at home was maybe six feet tall and had a wooden seat. This swing was nearly twice that tall and had a heavy rubber seat. I remember the different sensation we would experience on the larger swing, as if its size made it more "lumbering." You would complete the long arc forward and almost feel suspended in space, experiencing weightlessness for a few seconds. The swing would follow its path back and we would pump to bring it back forward again. We would lean out, to once again experience the freedom of being suspended above the ground.

I loved to swing. Come to think of it, I still do.

I would always race out of the room to get to the front of the line for the swings, often hearing a `"take it easy" or "let's not push" from Miss Waters as I shoved my way toward the front. Sometimes I would feel a bit guilty. Other times I didn't feel great about getting to the swing in front of everybody because my friends would have to wait for me to finish. The teacher would tell us when our time was up and we would stop swinging and the next person would take his turn. I would go off and play elsewhere.

But sometimes I would look back at the ones who were swinging after I had gotten off and they were trying new things, things I hadn't thought to try. Maybe they had figured out a way to synchronize their swing with the person next to them. They would laugh and yell to each other or maybe mirror one another's antics. Maybe they had figured out a neat way of jumping off the swing at the end of their turn, such as landing on both feet like a gymnast coming off the parallel bars. Maybe they were just laughing with each other and seeming to be having more fun than I had.

Let's face it: Being first is fun. You don't have to wait in line. Everyone has to watch, and wait, for you. You are a pioneer.

But going forward without a map or without a formula for success can be nerve racking. You are on your own: sink or swim. When you succeed, it can be great fun. You are the life of the party. By your own intelligence, hard work, and perseverance you can do great things. It doesn't get better than that.

I had the opportunity to lead a trade association as we developed a cross-industry B2B standard for trading billions of dollars worth of goods across multiple levels of the supply chain. I facilitated work across competitors to define our path forward as we debated the impact of various decisions. I had to establish trust with people who didn't know me and, almost by definition, certainly didn't have any reason to trust me. To a large degree, even through we were collaborating, I was still the enemy.

It was great fun being a pioneer. It turned out to be a real test of both technical knowledge and intriguing politics.

I also still have friendships borne out of working together with my competitors. Fundamentally, their issues were my issues and their trials were my trials. We all felt that way. We were careful not to do anything illegal or that would have the appearance of impropriety, but we also worked very closely together. We pushed ourselves to trust beyond the norm. We reached beyond our view, when our instincts screamed danger at us. We succeeded and we all learned from each other.

But when you fail, you are on your own. Your boss...the guy you thought was your cheerleader...lays the "problem" at your feet. He disassociates himself from your activities. So much for encouraging risk-taking! Being a pioneer is not without its own risks to ourselves.

So when should you be a pioneer?

❑ When B2B functionality is very closely aligned to your business strategy. This assumes you know "what you are about" (surprisingly often, that is not the case).

❑ When the reward far exceeds the risk of failure. If it is keeping you and your colleagues up at night with excitement, that is a clue you are on to something big!

❑ When your trading partners think it is exciting and want to help you. You have gotten their commitment to help with piloting, feedback, assessments, metrics, etc.

❑ When it is substantially different from what everyone else is thinking. When you can come out of nowhere to "capture the flag." Nothing is more exciting than knocking a market on its ear.

❑ When the risk of failure can be moderated. When it can be managed or accepted to some degree. I suggest you get this in writing from all parties, that they are willing to acknowledge and accept the risk.

But there are also advantages of waiting and watching. I am not talking about delaying until the optimal time of getting in the game. No, I am talking about using the time to become prepared; this is an equal activity level to pioneering.

It can be fine to let others go first. But figure out how to stay partnered with them. Stay involved and interested. Pick their brains at every opportunity. Cheer them on. Encourage them. And help them pick up the pieces if they should fall.

You need to be asking yourself the following questions to start down the road of successful waiting and watching:

❑ How can I add value to what someone else (such as my competitor) is doing?

❑ What are the "one off" opportunities? What can I pick up from other industries that could apply here?

❑ How can I do the exact same thing-- only faster, better, or cheaper?

❑ With whom can I connect who has had a somewhat similar challenge?

Once you have thoughts on how to proceed with any of the previous questions, set up short "deep dive" projects to evaluate them in full detail. Commit the resources needed to get after the roots. Time box the process (typically 30 days) and conclude them with some formal management review.

This type of activity is rarely done because the benefits are not yet in sight. And even when it is done, there is always the risk that things will change. Try this some time: ask your management to invest in something that may never pay out. Ask them for sizable funds to learn sometime in a preemptive fashion. They may get you a modest amount of seed resources to get something started. They may politely (or maybe less than politely) tell you to go away. This is a clear indication that B2B is not right for your company (or the company is not right for you) or whether you have more work to change your companies culture.

And when should you follow?

❑ When you can steal from the best.

❑ When you can learn from others without the risks that come with pioneering.

❑ When the risk of failure cannot be moderated or management isn't willing to "sign up" (i.e., more than lip service) to share the risks with you.

❑ When being first is of little or no value.

But don't try to be "half-pregnant." Attempting to be the "fast follower" always seems to satisfy management that they are doing the "reasonable and prudent" thing. You can hear it in a lot of ways: "Don't invest until the market has sorted out" or "Don't start until you have a tangible project where benefits are clear." The problem is you don't know what you don't know. You can't see enough to understand the benefits, much less be clear about them.

You can appear to "do the prudent thing" into extinction.

Fast follower strategies in B2B are normally high risk. People don't end up committing the necessary level of resources to "keep up." Mostly, people just find themselves flat footed at the bottom of the learning curve, while others (that choose to lead and commit the resources) get over the top of the curve and are gaining traction. It is impossible to gauge the time to begin to move forward aggressively because it is so easy to be disengaged and inattentive.

Sorry, "fast follower" strategy is an oxy-moron. Those who hope to be fast followers become "also rans." The lack of investment in getting ready to follow precludes your being fast. That is not a strategy. It is a tactic to avoid a strategy.

There is a time and place for being the pioneer; there is a time and place for being a follower. There is never a time for not getting prepared.

Being a pioneer or a follower is a conscious choice. Make it. Stick with it.

We should not only use all the brains we have, but all that we can borrow.

Woodrow Wilson

Stick Together

Grade school brought simple methods and simple rules. Stand in line when you wait for the bus. Play fair. Apply the Golden Rule. Hold hands when crossing the street. Stick together. Even today this is all good advice.

Our kindergarten teacher organized us together to keep us from wandering off-- both literally and figuratively. In doing so, she encouraged us to interact with one another. I remember being crowded together in awe as Miss Waters opened the petals of a flower before us. We had all seen flowers before and the boys largely ignored them--limiting their interest to pulling one apart petal by petal.

She gently showed us how the petals were attached and how the shapes allowed moisture and nutrients to draw down into the stalk. She told us that some flowers opened and closed on a regular basis to either protect themselves or to capture more sunlight. She even told us about meat-eating plants. Of course, we didn't figure flies were much in the way of meat!

She then asked us about flowers and some of the girls talked about the different smells and the variety of colors. I really hadn't thought much about that. When I listened to the girls talk, I began to see many things I hadn't observed before. We had a lot to learn about flowers. The girls knew the flowers that their mothers liked best and why. They knew the funny names for many of the flowers that our teacher brought in as examples. I was amazed by how much they knew and how much they could share.

eBusiness has more than its share of misinformation. Most of it is from "reliable sources." I have loved watching the statements from the "experts" about the life expectancy of Electronic Data Interchange (EDI) over the last few years. A few years ago it was "EDI is dead." Usually this was said by people who had something to sell-- either products or ideas. Then it was "EDI has only a few more years." Surprising, since it was already dead! More recently it has been "EDI and web-based B2B can go side-by-side." Does that mean they are both dead?

Nobody asked me if EDI was dead. Nobody asked anyone within my circle of eBusiness colleagues who have a wide range of experience in B2B technologies in a variety of companies and industries if EDI was dead. Most importantly, nobody asked my customers if EDI was dead. They're the ones who matter. They're are the ones who have collectively spent millions of dollars and countless hours putting together their EDI platforms and surrounding processes for support, problem resolution, and trading partner interaction. They are the ones who have streamlined their business processes and integrated EDI into their applications and systems.

The reality is that EDI has been growing at twice the rate of the economy in the last few years and doesn't really show signs of slowing down. If anything, many users' first look at the web or exchanges point out glaring deficiencies in those technologies. Once those glaring deficiencies are exposed, EDI doesn't look so bad after all. It may be old and stogy, but it works.

EDI does some things well and, at other things, it is dismal. The key is to match the tool to the requirements. B2B is not an "either-or" proposition; it is an "and-and-and." Sorry, one size does not fit all. One technology doesn't fit all, just as you will not find me hauling manure in my PT Cruiser!

The bottom line is that as long as trading partners see value in a technology, process, or method-- and it appears to be acceptable from a cost, speed, and complexity standpoint--

they will use it. It doesn't matter if it is smoke signals. And they will continue to use it until something substantially better comes along. Not just "faster, better, cheaper;" it has to exceed a certain threshold, far above that mark. A nebulous threshold called substantial improvement. The lesson is: don't race ahead by yourself to a new technology solution. You go down the road with others, specifically your customers and suppliers. When we implemented web-based tools for B2B, it was amazing how many companies didn't have web browsers and Internet connectivity at their employees' desktops. Many were concerned about the "distractions." Some were concerned about pornography and other inappropriate use. Some were concerned about the cost and others about security. It didn't matter that it was going to make life "faster, better, cheaper," there were still social and implementation cost issues at stake. There was still this threshold that needed to be exceeded before adoption would become a reality. It wasn't a matter of "could;" it was a matter of "would."

It is hard work taking customers through the process of alleviating their concerns. It takes education, training, trust, and socialization to help them through it. It takes them understanding that we are going to go through this together. That their success is my success and their failure is my failure.

Don't fall in love with a technology--"she will only break your heart." The best technology I ever saw for doing Advance Ship Notice was an inexpensive, special type of bar code reader. It would have cost our customers under $100 each in the mid-1980s for customers to "read" a special code attached to the bottom of their packing memo. We piloted with one customer. It worked well. However, it required a device to be hooked up to a PC to receive the data. Not all that many customers had PCs in those days and those who did were leery of hooking a device to it. The pilot was a success, but we were never able to implement the new technology. In other words, "The operation was a success, but the patient died."

New B2B technologies come along all the time and I get excited about them. But all need to go through an acceptance process before they can become viable in the marketplace. Sometimes that acceptance is allowing some "fringe" development to take place from a technology standpoint, to add security and safety to the method. All require socialization to gain acceptance. It requires working through the issues together and talking out the concerns and questions.

One of the most cost effective methods at a company I worked with has been a voice-response application that has been around for thirty years. Everyone has a telephone, so there is no additional cost to the user. The application is simple and direct and customers, frankly, have low expectations of it. By that I don't mean it can be of poor quality. I mean they don't expect us to be upgrading it with new features and elaborate functions very often. They don't anticipate that we will be changing it much at all. Change of this application is probably a bad sign in their minds. It works, it is stable, and it is reliable. Why fool with it? And that is quite alright with both of us.

On the other end of the spectrum we have been tinkering with public and private exchanges. Customers are largely not ready yet, so we have some time to find the right value equation. So what are the best forums for discussing where we need to be going next? Obviously, you want to keep in regular communication with your customers about these issues, but there are other forums to consider to gain alternative perspectives and to challenge our assumptions.

Industry-wide conferences and technology specific conferences are usually good for the interchange of ideas. You need to make sure they are not too vendor specific, especially where the vendor has a narrow band of "real" offerings. Many have a grand vision for how their product sets must work-- with only 30% of it really built out.

I prefer conferences that have many presentations by external, industry experts who have little to sell and plenty of real-live users. People who live and work in the trenches. People who "put it on the line" every day. People who live (and get fired) for their B2B decisions. They are the unsung heroes of B2B. They are not attracted to the limelight--they have to be dragged there. They're the ones who will give you the straight answers you need. They're the ones who will tell you the truth about the products and vendors.

America's SAP Users Group (ASUG) eCommerce group is one, for example. This is not the company SAP selling their vaporware (that's what their annual SAPPHIRE event is all about). This is real SAP users getting together to share their successes and failures in putting together their B2B solutions that integrate with their SAP back-end. This is real people helping other souls along the same road they have trudged. These folks "stick together" to help each other out, not just at conferences, but in email blast, web sites, and telephone calls.

Seminars can provide "intimate" contacts. Especially good are ones that are small and allow for a good deal of interchange between the speakers and the attendees. They can be low risk ways of being able to ask naive questions about how things work in a smaller, closer knit setting. Some of the best B2B seminars I have attended have had 15-20 people. They need to have sufficient breaks and discussion sessions, which will not only allow, but also facilitate, random questions and answers.

The learning at these sessions is not always from the instructor. It is from fellow attendees who are at (or just beyond) the point you are. I pay particular attention to what companies or industries these attendees represent and how far along in their implementations they may be. If it appears they are a "good match" for the information I think I may need, I will strike up a conversation and volunteer some information on my experience or approach. People generally always reciprocate. If not, I haven't invested too much. The amount of information that can be collected is striking.

Sometimes I gain far more from these "side bar" conversations than from the main seminar topic. Sometimes I gain friends who are willing to interact with me for years as our solutions go down separate paths and occasionally converge.

Cast a broad net with training. My boss in the late 1980s, Roger Rawden, had the best picture of training that I have ever run across. He insisted that his managers get out of the office one time a quarter for training. It could be a day or a week. The training needed to be only a "fair match"--in other words, it didn't have to have a "hard business case" that would be used on the particular job I was doing then, but it needed to be just a reasonable match for my jobs or some responsibility the team might acquire. When he proposed this to us, we were more concerned about our "Travel and Entertainment" budget, since we shared that performance expectation. But we soon learned there were low cost ways of doing training. We didn't need to fly cross-country and spend a week to get what we needed.

One part of this was just getting away from the office to gain a fresh perspective on the world. It was getting away from the daily grind to be able to tackle problems again in a different light. It is getting out with other companies that have successfully dealt with similar problems.

One two-day training I attended taught me some skills I use three or four times a year. Best $400 seminar I ever attended. In hindsight, it has saved them tens of thousands of dollars.

There are more opportunities today for training than there have ever been to get the training for B2B we need. But this typically excludes the connections we make with other companies doing similar projects. On-line training can supplement, not replace, "live" training. Why? It leaves out a valuable level of engagement with others. It bypasses the opportunity to stick together.

Huddled together, we figure B2B out. We learn from one another. We expand our thinking, beyond that of which we are individually capable. We cut through the misinformation and drive to the practical solution. We can do it time and again, by sticking together.

"Snowflakes are one of nature's most fragile things, but just look what they can do when they stick together."

Vesta M. Kelly

Be a Keen Observer

The "Dick and Jane" series of schoolbooks was in common use when I was growing up. There usually was a single sentence on a page with a drawing to illustrate what the words said on the opposing page. They had no plot and lots of action. They weren't "real" stories (Dick would have been running after Jane to kick her back) and it didn't tell the whole story (Dick really liked Jane), but something was always on the move. Even the dog.

Typically we would start off our reading slowly, but soon the boys in particular were racing ahead and through the book. We were more intent at getting through than doing a good job. Miss Waters was patient. She would help us by writing on the chalkboard any new words. She would ask each of us to read to her and sometimes we would read a sentence out loud to the whole class.

Sometimes we faltered and forgot what those words meant. Initially we would just memorize the words, but eventually we would learn to sound them out and compare them with other words we had seen earlier (like ballpark from having seen ball and park).

The girls generally were methodical, reading the words and carefully looking at the pictures. They were taking the time to associate the pictures with the words. They would even see some of the things in the pictures that didn't make sense ("Why weren't there any fences in the pictures?" and "Mom would kill us if we ran in our Sunday best shoes"). The girls would keenly observe the stories and decide what did and what did not "ring true."

It took diligence to think beyond the page. It was important to remember certain details to see how they "played out." We all began to think about what we read and heard. The authors intended these books to teach us to read, but they were also teaching us to think objectively.

While we didn't do any "substantial" reading in kindergarten, we were exposed to two things that could serve each of us all of our lives: reading and critical thinking.

During any stage of business upheaval, such as now while we are still in the formative years of eBusiness and while the "dot-com" implosion is behind us, we all need to be keen observers. We need to sharpen these skills even more than before. We need to methodically and thoroughly digest the information that is coming at us and do a better job of assessing its relevance and validity.

We need to be considering the hype that we are exposed to daily and to listen critically to the claims of success. We need to consider the source of information and reflect on "what they are selling to us and why."

We need to understand the different between teaching and selling. Weekly I am exposed to Webinars that are advertised as training vehicles, when in fact they are just the latest method of marketing. With training you should get a balanced view of products and services. You should be warned of the weak spots of a technology, method, or service. By nature, the marketing materials paint a rosy picture and comparisons are slanted to view the offering in the best possible light.

Many people flitter off to the latest technology, without understanding the potential impacts the technology will have. They gloss over the downsides. Their attitude is "we will deal with that when we get to it," when they need to deal with it mentally and emotionally right now. The web was viewed that way about five years ago. If it was "on the web" it was automatically good. It was automatically advanced and considered forward thinking.

You need to be discerning in taking in the information. It can bias your view from that point forward.

Know with whom you are dealing. Know "where they are coming from" seems too obvious, too simple. When you are talking to vendors it is pretty clear. They have a service or product to sell, and little is done externally to determine the next generation of offerings. So you know "up front" they are angling for the sale.

When you are talking to exchanges it may not be as clear. They can slip back and forth between their two roles: educator and vendor. This is especially true when we talk about channel related exchanges. I have yet to hear one of them say, "Use somebody else's offering, we ain't there yet." Instead, everything is within their domain. Or they have strategic partnerships that can "fill in the gaps." Or they are "in development" and the market isn't ready yet, "so just wait a bit."

But nearly all exchanges are in survival mode. They need the next sale to make it through the next quarter to make it to the next round of funding or sponsorship. They have no time to waste. They are angling for the sale more times than not. And what they have to sell is what they have on hand, not necessarily what you need. You need to be discerning.

Look for long lasting relationships. Strategic relationships can be instrumental to the success of your B2B program and in using a software suite. If you cannot get the attention of your vendor, you cannot be certain that their future offerings, services, and support model will align with your business strategy.

Of course, all vendors "talk" in terms of you being their strategic customer. But you need to be a keen observer to determine if their actions will mirror their "talk". Ask them for specific details on how they will do this and tell them specifically what your expectations of them should be. Then document your agreement and pull it out of the drawer frequently with your vendor to make sure you are staying on the right course.

We were in a "strategic partnership" to co-design a procurement offering. We had done an assessment of their current business model and software offering and it was shaky at best. They needed to beef up many of the features and functions. They sold us on a strategic relationship, where we would co-design the next generation of software. However, their vision of co-design and develop and our vision were severely misaligned. We paid for a great deal more of their labor than we had expected. And when they got to the next generation of product, they had gone in a totally different direction, without considered much of our input. In hindsight we hadn't laid out the specific expectations of both companies.

But we also hadn't been keen observers of their behaviors when they had droves of employees on our premises. We hadn't, for example, recognized that the people "on site" where not their most senior development staff. We hadn't recognized they were not getting back to us very quickly on feedback we had provided. We were cutting them too much slack, in thinking our feedback was winding its way through their channels. These should have been telltale signs that things were amiss.

Because we hadn't been keen observers early on in the process, we hadn't laid the correct foundation for what "co-design" really meant. We paid the price for our blunder.

This should not be construed to imply you don't want strategic relationships. They can be very valuable and save you money and time to market. But we need to ask ourselves, "How well does this vendor understand my eBusiness strategy?" and "How much does he care?" Actions make speak louder than words, but you have to be listening to both.

Strive for balance. Finding balance requires diligence and attention. It requires patience and a steady hand. It requires keen observations.

If it sounds easy, take another look. Remember, the technology is the easy part. Don't look for what "could be done." That's too easy. Look beneath the surface to see what level of acceptance you can drive. Read between the lines. Look for what "rings true" and what does not.

Don't look for "conceptual" acceptance. Look for willingness to put down hard dollars and other resources. Balance what you are hearing from your vendors and what you are hearing from your trading partners. Think critically and listen to yourself as well. Don't get carried away and enthusiastic until after you have seen the alignment.

It still takes diligence to think beyond the page. It is still important to remember the details and reflect on how they can "play out" in the business world.

Think critically when the hype and your enthusiasm and emotions are at the zenith. Be a keen observer.

Never trust the judgment of an enthusiastic man; never trust the promises of a lazy one.

Mason Cooley

Listen to Instructions

Early one day we were sitting at tables coloring with crayons on foot square pieces of glossy, white paper, which had been taped to the table. Unlike the way we usually colored in kindergarten, we didn't try to make a picture of something. The teacher had instructed us to use bold, dramatic colors to make a design consisting of shapes of bright color on the page--rectangles, squares, and circles. We made some very interesting designs. Next, she instructed us to put on the paint shirts (old, long sleeved shirts our dads had worn out) which we had been told to bring into the class early in the school year. Miss Waters told us we would put black paint on top of our design, right up to the edge of the paper.

At first the paint just seemed to bead up on the colors. I thought, "This isn't going to work." She told us to be persistent and use more paint to continue to cover the paper until it was completely covered in black. Now this didn't seem to make sense to me, but I did as I had been told. While we were still painting, Miss Waters went from table to table placing in the center a pile of paper clips which had one end bent back and straightened out.

She told us that we wouldn't need these right now. Actually, I think told us not to touch them, but since we were the first table, how could I possibly resist? While she was passing out the paper clips, she explained that after lunch, when the paint was "good-and-dry," we would scratch off some of the paint to expose the crayon beneath.

Wow! I wanted to see that right now! I grabbed a paper clip and began to scratch. The paper was still saturated with paint and I easily scratched through and tore the paper. Great patches of black paint began oozing onto the table, onto the floor, and soaking through my paint shirt. Not only was my art project destroyed, I was a mess.

Defect and rework are killers to eBusiness projects. In our anxiety to get the product out the door or the project to completion, we forget the fundamentals of business. It all starts out with a good design. It needs to be well thought out and viewed from the users' perspective. We need to listen to the users to give us instruction on how they can use the tools we are building. This is an interactive process of getting the design right.

I like to interview design people or document the process flows. I prefer to use highly descriptive, text-based use cases to drive the functional design. These supplement, but do not replace graphic diagrams of the process flows and other tools to detail the data mapping and data field requirements. I likely will also generate "swim-lane" diagrams to talk about the interaction between the users and the application.

The next step is to get a larger community of internal associates to review the use cases. These sessions usually amaze me. It doesn't matter how short or how long we may have been discussing a design, there are always different assumptions and expectations on how a web application will operate. Usually, at this initial session (provided you have allowed adequate time) we can sort much of the conflict and lack of understanding of the design.

Typically it is still only a rough cut of the design. Things will need to ferment a bit and people will need to withdraw to come to terms with the changes. You will need to get this larger, internal team together once again (and maybe multiple times) to get to the 90% of design state.

Think you are done? Not even close. Next you need to generate what my colleague, Vince Bianchi, termed "dirty pictures." These are drawings of how the screen layouts will look. Graphic design people with experience in user interface are invaluable in working through the flow of screens and in making them as "intuitively obvious" as possible. I define a well designed screen as one that "instructs" itself: in other words, a user can look at the screen and figure out how to make it work without additional aids, such as user manuals or on-line help screens. The dirtier these pictures are the better. By that I mean "back of envelope" screen shots are better than an elaborately done, mock-up of the application with full, polished graphics. Why?

There are three reasons. First, you want to give the user the understanding that you are not done and that you want their active participation in this work. Everyone likes to be consulted early. It makes them feel valued and included. It tells them that you recognize that they are essential to your design and that they are the principle reason for doing this work. It is also a good time to ask for their participation in piloting the application.

Second, you want to work quickly. Waiting while the graphic design is presented and debated with marketing, brand management, legal, etc., can be very time consuming. Third, this is probably throwaway work.

Do it right the first time. A well-crafted business and eBusiness strategy is the start of your instruction. It needs to articulate the value not only to your company, but also throughout the value chain. Your suppliers and service providers should be in alignment with your strategy. They should see the value of their participation in the improvement of the overall business.

If they cannot see that value, one of two things is wrong. Either your strategy is not sufficiently broad to encompass their business direction and desires or you have the wrong partners-- you are headed in one direction and they are headed in another. Your path forward is clear: change the strategy or change the partners.

One of our value strategies is customer self-service. This means giving our customers features that enable them to perform functions on their timeline. If that means on a Sunday afternoon they want to be able to place orders, that is fine with us. If the customer wants to track their shipments "on-line, anytime, anywhere," that's great with us as well. But if our carriers don't create and maintain web sites that are aligned with that vision, or if they are not willing to provide the data back to us in a useful, timely manner, then their business vision and ours are no longer in alignment. We either get aligned or get a new carrier or get a new strategy.

To do otherwise and, thereby, put together an application that "makes do" with the limitations we just accept, is foolhardy and will ultimately dissatisfy our customers and ourselves. You need to challenge this thinking. It risks getting black paint all over you.

Once you have determined what your strategy is, once you have solidified it in your heart and mind, it becomes the rough draft of your instruction manual.

We still have a way to go before we are done. We need to validate the model against customers' desires and wishes on two levels: strategy and application.

The strategy level aligns their business goals with our business goals. It is best to send out feelers to determine the level of acceptance and likely issues your strategy will raise. Then formalize the strategy. Only finalize and publish your strategy after you have achieved alignment with your customers. If you get the "cart before the horse," you risk getting black paint all over yourself.

Now you can begin working on your B2B application. Your instruction manual is not quite done. It is neither polished nor perfect. It will still need to be tweaked as you learn more. However, you have arrived at the point where you can validate the model against the customers' desires and wishes on an application basis.

Listening to feedback interactively. The feedback that you collect from users will challenge you to do things differently and will result in a different design than you had anticipated. What they will give to you are instructions on how your application should operate. It still needs to work within the context of your "instruction manual," but it will be different in many ways from your original concept of how things should work.

Each of these "design and listen" loops tells us more and more about how the B2B application needs to work. Each is a lesson to us. We need to assimilate this instruction and "bring it to life" on our web pages and other B2B applications.

As we do so, we inch closer and closer to the final design. We inch closer and closer to a full understanding of the functions and limitations the application will have. We inch closer and closer to understanding what our strategy means in the real world.

We need to use these loops primarily to sharpen our focus and limit, not expand, functionality. We use this to pare down the design to a crisp, clean process. This is not about adding "bells and whistles." B2B drives us to the essential portions of the business process. Done right, it rips out "dancing banners" and leaves us with the bare bones of "getting the job done."

Work to eliminate data entry and to reduce errors. In moving to electronic processes we want to eliminate manual data entry. You want to push as much of this to the beginning of the process and pass the data on electronically to subsequent processes and business systems applications. Those systems applications may be at your trading partner's site. It doesn't matter who saves the labor. The elimination or streamlining of the process is the key objective. If the elimination of data entry for one trading partner is merely passed off to another trading partner, no improvement to the information cycle has really occurred. Go back to the drawing board and see if there are ways of eliminating the work process.

You can also move responsibility for errors to the person most likely to create them. Make the person generating the errors also the one most impacted by the incorrect data. As we moved to web order entry, we enabled some customers to do their own drop shipments. Now the bad address they type in or the inadequate telephone number they supply can come back to haunt them.

To automate a broken manual process is foolish. It is asking for a bath of "black paint." Yet, almost every day someone comes forward with something they want to move to the web when they haven't accessed the manual process.

Both trading partners should share the benefits in proportion to their investment. That investment can be either capital or on-going costs. This can be a situation of "you scratch my back, I'll scratch your back." Look for opportunities to trade off benefits: you do something that benefits your trading partner in exchange for something that benefits you.

Typically the buyer loves to have electronic invoices. It helps them with three-way matches of data-- matching the invoice with the purchase order with the delivery documentation. Many companies have their accounts payable and purchase order applications in the same systems or systems that are closely linked. Being able to provide the invoice allows two of the three matches to occur in a less manual manner. Billers love to have electronic payments. It streamlines handling and reduces the delivery-to-payment cycle and improves day's sales outstanding (DSO).

Remarkable as it may seem, sometimes you can give away something that costs you little or nothing. Other times it allows you to give away something you really want the customer to have anyway.

One time we "wanted" to put order acknowledgment information in the customer's hands. But we gave it to the customer with the stipulation that we would only give it to them if they promised to look at the information before calling us on the status of their shipments. Amazingly, it substantially reduced routine calls to customer service. The overall call centers' number of calls dropped by eleven percent! The substantial call reduction equated to a similar reduction in customer service support costs.

You need to listen carefully to your trading partners to discern what they value. Like the colors in the art design, following instructions allows the beauty of your design to shine through, without making a mess of things.

"I like to listen. I have learned a great deal from listening carefully. Most people never listen."

Ernest Hemingway

Competition

Competition comes to us naturally. All boys want to be the fastest on the playground and highest on the swings. The girls in our class wanted to be the most friendly or most popular. It is part of our nature to strive to be "the best" and to measure ourselves against others.

It wasn't something we really needed to be taught. But it did need to be honed and channeled. Much of our educational life is geared to sharpening us to live in a world where we first competed for school grades, then slots at colleges and universities and scholarship funds, and then in the job market.

In kindergarten we honed the social skills that would make us successful in getting our education off to a good start. We prepared for the tasks ahead of us. We were evaluated on our successes and failures individually. Even then we were striving to paint the best picture, we were striving to stand out in the eyes of our parents and in front of our siblings.

In our neighborhood we competed for friends and their playtime. There were plenty of other activities we could be doing and many of them were competitive. When we were with our friends we played "Cowboys and Indians" to see which side would win. We would play "Cops and Robbers" to see if the bad guys could outsmart the good guys. We would play Capture the Flag and Over the Line to see who was best.

Gary Oien and I were always racing against each other. Sometimes he would win and sometimes I would win. We were pretty evenly matched physically. One time his mother bought him some high topped "Red Ball" sneakers. They were really neat and I was sure there was no way that I would be able to keep up with him. I was really going to have to give it all my effort to beat him and those "Red Ball" sneakers. But I was determined and I did beat him and when I did, I really rubbed it in.

He said his shoes were still stiff from being new and to watch out. He took off his shoes to show me his blisters. While I kept beating him, I knew I had to keep pushing myself if I was going to continue to beat him and he knew that as well. I did continue to beat him, but not for long. Once he had gotten his shoes broken in, we were competitive once again.

I was a better runner for having pushed myself. When he ran against me, I became stronger--and so did he.

And when my shoes were well worn and needed replacing, I had something to consider.

As Hewlett-Packard and Eastman Kodak converged on the same competitive marketplace they both announced their intention to be "King of the Hill" in digital photography-- okay, not in so many words, but you get the picture.

Both are very capable technology companies with a rich history of innovation and brand excellence. Both have poured billions of dollars into the science and research needed in this market. Both companies came to the "hill" with high expectations of themselves and a keen understanding of the potential. Both companies came to the "hill" with their own bias. I am sure the Hewlett-Packard team was thinking, "If they only knew what they don't know about printing technologies" and the Kodak team was thinking, "If they only knew what they don't know about color science."

And this goes on in every country, marketplace, and technology in the world.

There is a great deal to learn from your competitors. The quickened pace of B2B has compelled us to act. We have recognized the peril of being left in the dust. We see how industries and companies have changed. We are aware of companies that have risen to stardom in the Internet age. We have seen others fall by the wayside to be broken up or picked apart.

B2B has increased the visibility of what companies are doing. Now, companies proudly display on their web sites their activities and direction. Now they trumpet their capabilities. No longer is what they are doing behind closed doors. The web browser has opened a new view into our competition. New relationships are proclaimed in product press releases. A series of browser search capabilities can bring you a goldmine of competitive information. New tools for understanding the competition are readily at hand.

It is enlightening to take a look at a problem from another viewpoint. Looking at our competitors gives us a slightly different view of the world and our business problems. But only slightly different. Look at something about ten feet away with only your right eye and notice the details in the background and their relation to other objects. Now look only through your left eye and notice how the details in the background and their relation to other objects have shifted. It is similar to the way we see things differently when we view the world from our competitions perspective. Many things are similar and familiar. But many things have changed.

They compete in the same channels and with the same customers. But they may attack problems in a different way, if for no other reason than that they have "you" with whom to contend.

Competitors come at the markets in very predictable ways. They establish thought patterns and ways of operating that are consistent over time. It is only with great turmoil and consternation that they move away from the "mold." This is an advantage as we look at the competitive landscape. It is usually only with either 1) the massive and dramatic change of leadership at the top (normally from outside) or 2) when the business is at great peril, there are few other options, and survival is at stake. But there is nothing like a wounded animal to demonstrate unpredictable behaviors.

They may choose to head off in different directions to see if you can keep up. One of my competitors has gotten closely linked with a software company that makes supply chain tools. Up until this time they have chosen to allow us to lead and either stub our toes or reap the lion's share of the rewards from leading. They were content to come in later, mirror our processes, and take a small portion with reduced risk. But maybe not any longer.

Now they are looking to change the dynamics in the market by getting closer to a few, key retail customers and linking together with them seamlessly. They are attempting to steal away a few of "the best" with their B2B initiatives. But can they sustain this change? Can they turn this into a new model for their business?

I need to be able to respond to that and am using B2B tools to do so. I am also choosing to go about the problem in a different way. The linking with my customers will be different, less intrusive, less demanding, and, hopefully, a less expensive way to create a similar competitive advantage. Benchmarking and studying my competitor helps me understand how he is competing with me. It helps to know the questions I need to be asking my customers and myself.

Frequently customers will raise the stakes concerning what is taking place with your competitors. They do that for two reasons: the carrot and the stick. When it is the "carrot," they are signaling where your competitor is "off the mark" and you have an opportunity. Of course, they are telling you this for their own reasons--they want you to respond in a certain way so your competitor will be forced to follow suit. When it is the "stick," they are signaling where your competitor is "on the mark" and you had better play catch-up and play it <u>now</u>.

Have a great deal of respect for your competitors. Just like when I was running against Gary, we need to respect our competition. They are bright people. They have the same hopes and desires for their families that we do. They have bills to pay and mouths to feed. They hone their skills based on their assessment of our strengths and weaknesses. They target our soft underbelly. They target the "chinks" in our armor. Those are the narrow openings, cracks and fissures in our business process. For example, there are places were the sales teams and the finance teams come together. Where differences in internal operational teams' responsibilities cause them to have different objectives. These different business objectives cause us to give mixed messages to our customers.

I was on the receiving end of one of those mixed messages. A vendor had offered a service to us for a fraction of the price we were paying. Furthermore, they offered this service at this price across our whole business. And it was an industry-wide deal that we were negotiating. That was wonderful for us. What they hadn't counted on was the amount of existing business this offer would be impacting. They were thinking about a narrow swatch of the business--one channel. They didn't understand that we couldn't break out this one channel by itself effectively. We handled the US business all in one fashion. When they started understanding, they realized the vendor they were displacing at a fraction of the cost was largely themselves!

That's when their finance people got involved and their internal wrangling took place. This went on for months. It is where their "chink" showed up. What they had placed before us in "black and white" was a large hit on their revenue; it wasn't just Kodak (where I was working at the time), it was also 3M, Agfa, and Dupont.

They were in a position where they had served to themselves a large competitive problem. They could probably have backed away from the deal and been the laughing stock of their industry and created for themselves a new competitive problem. After all, we easily could have "shopped" the same deal to their competitors.

Or they could move forward with the deal, save face, and take away the competitive threat. In the end, they recognized the opportunity was in moving forward with what they had offered. Better to have a larger piece of a smaller pie than no pie at all.

Competition is not something to be feared. The worst situations in which a company I worked for has put itself is when management attempted to instill fear in the employees based on the abilities of the competition.

There have not been many of these situations, but in every instance it had the reverse of the desired effect. It was intended to make us work harder and smarter. Instead, it generated a great deal of rumor, innuendo, and distraction. The discussion around the water cooler didn't help the situation. It fueled itself to an unrealistic pitch. We were more afraid of their shadow than ever before. We started to mirror the other company's behaviors and designs. We concentrated more on their strengths than our strengths. We failed to concentrate on their weaknesses.

No longer could we differentiate ourselves.

Business is a race. B2B is an enabler to "better, faster, cheaper" ways of doing business. The web can be both a tool for accessing our competition and for beating them in the marketplace. We need to be watchful and aware of what the competition is doing. We need to do this out of respect instead of fear. We need to access how we can best compete and take clearest advantage. Our competition can show us part of the way if we are watchful and astute.

> *"You can discover what your enemy fears most by observing the means he uses to frighten you."*
>
> *Eric Hoffer*

High Touch

She stood next to me while I awkwardly handled the scissors. First Miss Waters watched to see how I managed them on my own. They were not the same type of scissors my mother used. Instead of being large, they were closer to the size of my hands. That was pretty neat at first glace.

But they didn't seem to be very well made. They were very flimsy, actually. They had a little rivet in the middle where the blades rotated that was a bit wobbly. The blades tended to separate and, instead of cutting the paper, just wedged the paper between them. My mother's scissors were hefty and precision engineered. These scissors were very lightweight by comparison. And what was the deal with the rounded front end? How was I going to ram through the paper to cut out large holes?

She then came to me and formed the fingers of my right hand into the finger holes of the scissors. She held my left hand as I held the orange construction paper and pulled the paper tight against the blade. She had me put pressure on the scissors to cut. More pressure than I had to use with my mother's well engineered, heavy duty, precision blades. Together we cut out a pumpkin. Cool! Then another. Cool! Soon, I could cut them out by myself. Way cool!

When we try out new skills, we all need reassurance. Do you remember the days when your father or uncle or an older friend taught you how to ride a bike? How about the first time you caught a baseball or swung a bat? How did you do?

None of us is an instant expert. When we were young, we weren't expected to be. All of us fell down or missed the ball more than once. If we were lucky we had someone to work with us, to encourage us, and to be patient with us.

My father spent endless hours playing catch with me. At the time, I was sure he had better things he could be doing. Only when I became a father myself did I understand that there wasn't anything more important he could be doing. He did it because I needed it and asked him for help.

Why is it different in the eBusiness world? We all seem to want to be seen as experts. We don't want to show how little we know. We pride ourselves in being professionals. Yet, in our day-to-day activities, we mostly do things that don't hone our professional skills. We fill out forms and schedules, revise plans, and make proposals. As companies, in our short horizon thinking, we invest the minimal amount. And it shows.

Profitability, being measured as a ratio of income against expense, leads us to think in terms of getting profitable in the fastest way possible and not the best possible way. It never considers the long haul. It never considers that we could leap frog someone else. It doesn't easily think in terms of profitability for many quarters in a row.

The amount we need to learn in eBusiness is incredible. We face either a barrage of misinformation or a desert of non-information. So how do we learn? We get conflicting information and skewed viewpoints. For example, to speed up websites many vendors have pushed for placing business rules and master data out at the front end (on the website). This is effective in the one objective of speed. It is ineffective when considering quality and consistency that comes with an integrated solution. It introduces other factors that are equally important, such as new errors based on inconsistent data and complexity based on the need for replication of data. You certainly are not going to get real downside information from the vendor who has a vested interest in you seeing only one part of the problem. You only get those truths from others who have dealt with the issues and understood the tradeoffs. That gives us a depth of information and an independence that provides balance in our evaluations.

We need to get outside our own four walls to see what is happening in the world. When did we begin considering training and research as a necessary evil? We tend to have a skewed view of both that is directly portioned to its cost. The lowest cost training typically is "on the job" training. If we support that activity with adequate time and resources, it can be of great benefit. If we set aside adequate time to develop training materials, orient mentors, and demonstrate management support, it can be very effective. It is only effective, however, when someone in your company has 1) a high level of expertise, 2) an ability to train others, 3) a love for passing along knowledge, and 4) management support, demonstrated in a willingness to commit the time, resources, and, in the short term, degradation of performance that will be necessary. All four are critical.

Usually "on the job" training is an excuse for not doing things correctly, either in planning or executing our training plans. On the job training becomes "catch as catch can" training.

Too bad we don't measure training against its value. We don't set up adequate or accurate measures of the effectiveness of training. Too frequently training is considered a luxury, treated as a non-essential. Too much training is considered a waste, but how do we know how much is enough? Too little training is somehow considered a prudent investment! Do we value just allowing employees the time to learn things that are not obviously connected? It happens, but it is rare. Do we fly them off to conferences and seminars without having done a highly detailed business case? Not normally. At one company, they expected all employees to get forty hours of training, yet they counted things like "learned to use the phone system" or "training on how our benefits package works." All these things are important to know, but they will hardly create a sustainable, competitive advantage using eBusiness. And there is so much to be learned.

Only the wise set aside their egos and ask for help. I am expected to be an expert in my field. After all, doesn't my company pay me to bring forward the right expertise in my niche? However, my field is shifting so dramatically and so quickly that what I learn today may not be relevant tomorrow.

It is like a doctor a few years out of medical school. If he hasn't stayed engaged in learning, in a few years he isn't practicing the latest in medicine. Part of this is setting aside our need to be perceived as the expert and asking for help.

I used to work in a library. I learned wonderful things, but the best skill I learned was in knowing how to get information I need. This has served me well in eBusiness. As the Internet has become a pervasion business tool, it has brought with it a mixed blessing...a plethora of information consisting of a wealth of good information and the curse of a similar volume of bad information. The key is in understanding "which is which."

Part of that understanding is instinct and part of it is determining who can guide you. Generally, if it seems too good to be true, it is. I have had numerous occasions where people, generally in sales, have told me the dramatic savings I could achieve with their products or services, yet they haven't taken the time to understand my business drivers or costs. They haven't understood my issues before trying to solve my problems. They haven't been watchful or patient to understand where I needed help. I have also had wise counsel on how to look at problems and understand the direction the world is going. These have been extremely valuable, but, unfortunately, also rare.

We need to set low expectations of ourselves as we learn skills or use new tools. There can be multiple levels of low expectations for us. We need to clearly anticipate and give ourselves adequate time for learning new things. Frequently we try to learn new skills while we keep the rest of our job running. This doesn't do justice to either the new area or the old job. So plan for adequate time and attention; some of this is setting expectations with our bosses and some is setting expectations for ourselves. Expect that there will be two elements of any training-- the more formal component and the time needed to apply what you have learned to real life situations. This may not be particularly easy with eBusiness activities.

I attended classes about ten years ago on Internet EDI. This was driven by a number of customer inquiries and my general interest in the subject. Having taken the training, I immediately did an assessment of what we would need to do to build this capability. Since that time I haven't done much directly with what I learned because interest has waned. Ideally, I would have had one or more potential projects "in the pipeline" ahead of the trainings so I could have applied the training with the "doing." This doesn't mean the training was a total loss as I have been able to apply what I have learned to other aspects of eBusiness. What I learned that could be applied elsewhere had nothing to do with technology; it had everything to do with human nature.

We need to set low expectations of rookies. That isn't to say we set low expectations on the quality of their work nor the effort they put into their training. It is that we set low expectations on how quickly and how much they can learn in a particular span of time. We shouldn't assume that they would come back from a seminar or class and have the answers. We should expect that they would come back with new levels of inquisitiveness and new sources for research and answers. A diamond is not created by occasional pressure; it takes constant and consistent pressure. The same applies for rookies to eBusiness. Expect slow, but continual progress. This includes how we deal with our customers and suppliers.

Managers of B2B organization need to offer help, provide "space," and provide "blocking" where necessary. We need to learn the right level of involvement with others. The parable of "giving someone a fish" versus "teaching someone to fish" needs to be paramount in my mind.

We need to be models of patience with those who work for us and for those we mentor. But we also shouldn't confuse patience with the earnest desire to improve and accomplish.

All B2B workers need to seek help from those more experienced, both within and outside their organizations. They need to be patient with themselves and other they encounter. Their mindset needs to be: "We are all in this together." That extends out to our trading partners as well as our co-workers.

Fundamentally, we need to put on "high tough" thoughtware. We need to thinking "How can I help others along?" That's the way Miss Waters did it. She waited patiently to see how she could help. Then she nurtured us along until we could successfully handled things on our own. She had the heart to help us. High touch was her focus.

Patience is a necessary ingredient of genius.

Benjamin Disraeli, Earl of Beaconsfield (1804-1881)

Helping Others

I always liked "sharing time." I guess I still do. It was the most interesting part of our week in kindergarten.

Everyone was asked to bring something special to class. Of course, "special" is relative and we would see a wide range of items. Most things were interesting, some things were "Whew, what did you have to do to get one of those?," and other things were "yawners" (like the girls' favorite dolls).

Each person would spend about five minutes sharing something special about his or her life. It could be something large or small. It could be a thing, a person, an activity, or an event. It didn't matter.

I remember bringing a glass dome to class. When you turned it over pieces of plastic simulated snow falling on a house in the middle of the forest. I'm not sure why I liked it, maybe because it was different. This was really a simple activity, yet we were exposed to something new and different in our world.

I found out things about my friends that I had never known before. How about Karen's butterfly collection-- gosh, some of those butterflies were monsters! I had never seen anything like that before. In fact, I remember feeling scared looking at a butterfly that was the about the size of my dad's two hands. There was something eerie in the thought of something that gentle, yet that large, landing on me. That night I had a nightmare about a monster butterfly. I was glad there was a pin through that guy!

Who would have thought that Norman would have such an extensive collection of baseball cards? That encouraged me to start a collection of my own.

It is enlightening to take a look at a problem or opportunity from another viewpoint. We tend to get wrapped up in our own little world and don't look beyond our four walls. In the heat of battle, we don't tend to look to the soldier next to us to see the struggles he endures. We plow through situations by ourselves. We think we are the only one with a problem or the only one who has experienced our particular problem.

This is especially true when it comes to eBusiness. There is so much for us to learn and, frankly, few resources from whom to learn. We get a barrage of magazine articles that hit eBusiness from the technical angle, but hardly any resources that provide what we really need. That is like learning to drive based on understanding how the engine operates. While that may be interesting, it hardly places us behind the wheel. It neglects the skills of anticipating another driver's moves or the social skills of letting someone merge into your lane.

The same applies for books that target managers on setting a "top-down" eBusiness strategy, but little applies to the guys in the trenches.

It starts with our being receptive to helping others. Being receptive to helping others begins with the right perspective: "We are all in this together."

It is obviously important to work closely with your trading partners and internal service providers. In being receptive to helping others, they recognize they can come to you for assistance. In working with customers, you will have the opportunity to see the world through their eyes and understand their concerns. This gives you a "leg up" on proactively working through their stumbling blocks-- real and perceived. You will be able to monitor their progress and reinforce your message over a period on time.

Helping and training your own employees is also valuable. It increases your customer's base of support. Frequently employees' inexperience will show. They may even be threatened by your efforts to move your company to B2B. So be it. You are in a perfect position to help them understand what is occurring in the world around them.

They may not like what they see coming their way, but they will likely recognize two things: first, it is unavoidable and, second, it is not something you personally are doing "to them." Once they recognize that their company cannot be competitive without B2B, they can begin to see what new role they can play, either inside or outside of their current job or company.

They can personally access the new skills and training they will require to be successful in the future. They might not like the change they may view as being "imposed upon them." That's only natural. But they may be able to see a larger and more negative change that is "looming" if their company doesn't become more competitive. Either way, change is going to have an impact on their lives.

By putting aside our competitive natures, we can sometimes learn a great deal. Some of the best sharing times I have had have been with my competitors. I ran a sub-committee on technical EDI standards for an international trade association, which involved working with representatives from all my major competitors. I talked with them about the issues we were facing, the personalities of the people with whom we were working, the things that I had done that were successful, and the things that had not worked. Initially, they were quite surprised by my comments and how forthright I was in speaking with them. When I met hesitation or outright resistance, I was just persistent in passing along information and the experiences I had had. Counter-intuitive, isn't it?

Over time, they began sharing their approaches and insights with me and identifying what had worked well for them. Since I was interacting with many competitors and each of them was engaged only with me, we experienced different degrees of success. When I was approaching 85% of my customers fully implemented, they were hitting around 50-60%. For many reasons those were some of the most fun and rewarding times I have had in my business career.

Sharing with others allows us to observe new things or "refresh" our experience. Many times I have had colleagues come to me with a problem. Frequently, they are encountering something I had been through years before. Talking through the problem, listening to their questions, or hearing their concerns reinforces those activities that led to earlier successes.

Contrary to popular belief, you don't have to know everything to get started. In reality, you only need to know one thing that would help someone else. Sometimes you can just share a recent experience. Other times, you may just want to ask others to share something with you.

Facilitate learning sessions. Frequently you can host learning sessions with customers and suppliers. Often you can get software consultants or vendors to discuss their products and services; they are usually eager to increase exposure. What better way than through their current customers? You need to clearly identify the topic and set expectations, as these are not sales pitches. They may create interest that would lead to a sales opportunity, but that is not the primary focus.

You can establish classroom activities and conduct mini-seminars on a topic of interest to your customers. That can be done in a non-threatening, supportive atmosphere.

I also like to conduct "tea leaf" sessions. In this activity you get people together to reflect on what they are observing in the marketplace and are hearing from their customers. In effect, you set the mood for considering what the future may bring and what needs to be done to prepare. These can also be very helpful in collecting competitive information and in understanding the concerns of others. It can also lead to additional follow-up opportunities, such as seminars, classroom teaching, articles for trade journals, emails and webzines, and webinars.

Try some writing or "speaking engagements." People are always interested in hearing what others have to say. Just share your story-- what you have learned along the way, what you have accomplished and your trials in the process.

Speaking at eBusiness conferences, customer meetings and small, local "events" (such as local eBusiness associations, Rotary International, or Kiwanis clubs) can be rewarding. If you aren't sure whether speaking is your "cup of tea," try sitting on panels or interviews.

If you are really uncomfortable with public speaking, then try writing monthly email "blasts", blogs or webzines for a small trade journal in your area of interest. Or volunteer for a phone interview with the editor of an eBusiness magazine that covers topics that interest you. Normally, you can locate the editors' names and email addresses in magazines or web sites.

There are opportunities at the local, regional, national and international level-- whatever suits your "comfort level," tastes, and finances. My favorite happens to be international conferences that are mostly "vendor-neutral." International doesn't mean having to speak before a cast of thousands. It does mean having different cultures and a wide angle of the business audience.

The old adage "what goes around, comes around" still applies: for better or worse. Make it a better world by sharing your insights and knowledge with others. Give without the anticipation of receiving back and you will be richly rewarded, sometimes in unexpected ways.

Try not to become a man of success, but rather try to become a man of value.

Albert Einstein

Walk In The Other Guy's Shoes

There was no doubt about it. It was going to happen again. All the guys knew something bad was coming. We eyed one another. We could tell it in her voice-- sugar sweet and higher pitched than usual. No doubt about it. Miss Waters was going to make us do "girlie things" again.

There was nothing worse than "girlie things." Last time she had us cutting out paper clothing to dress paper dolls. Yuck. The girls loved this stuff. They would patiently color coordinate the clothing and make matching patterns. With purses and hats and high heels. Necklaces and diamond rings. Belt buckles and bouquets. Could there be anything more boring?

For the guys it was white tee shirts, black tennis shoes, and blue jeans. We were done in two seconds. The girls could spend hours doing this junk. Of course, we would have to wait for them to finish. Here we go again.

Miss Waters pulled out a large bed sheet. She asked us to stand in the center of the classroom. She started by taking away all the fun, "Okay, boys, no rough housing." She had us doing some crazy things like bumping into each other (without rough housing, no less) and pressing our faces against the tautly held bed sheet. The girls liked this because they would squeeze up with their boyfriends. Double yuck.

We were getting a little rambunctious, so Miss Waters told Ronnie that he was excused from this activity and he sat down to watch. Miss Waters was always "playing favorites" with Ronnie. Hey, what do I have to do to get excused? We were always getting hurt, so maybe if I limped like Ronnie I could get out of doing this thing. When Ronnie walked he would swing his hip forward and catch himself with all his weight on top of his leg. He was always getting out of doing stuff in class. He was also "too delicate" to play at recess, so we never asked him to play with us.

When we finally finished, I went over and sat next to Ronnie. He was telling me how he wished he could have played with the bed sheet with us. Yeah, right. I was mad. I asked him how come he always got out of things. "Miss Waters must be in love with you," I snapped. "You always weasel out of the bad stuff."

He had tears in his eyes. He didn't say anything. He just reached down and pulled up his pant leg. I was shocked by what he showed me. His right leg was as skinny as a broomstick. He quietly explained it was a birth defect and that he never would have the chance to play like the rest of his classmates did.

I didn't know what to say. I know I never saw Ronnie in the same way again. I even learned it was okay to play with him on the playground. He wasn't so bad or so delicate after all.

It is enlightening to take a look at a problem from another viewpoint. Sometimes what comes from that is unexpected; other times it confirms our own thinking. There is value either way. At times having missed the obvious clues shocks us. Other times we are enlightened with things that we will carry with us the rest of our business lives.

One customer introduced me to the concept of "value need" (versus "value add"). We think in terms of adding the next feature or function, without necessarily understanding what the impact, or value, will be from the customer's standpoint. The world is full of examples of "new and improved" features being added to products or services. The Ford Edsel was packed with the latest devices. It was a virtual cornucopia of "new and improved" features. Many of these were not highly valued by potential customers. Others were poorly designed or engineered. We need to understand how much (or how little) trading partners value our services and offerings. We need to differentiate in our minds their "wants" from their "needs." We only get that when we go beyond just asking them to discover the underlying situation.

We also need to help the customer move from the paradigms of the present to see the future with different eyes. For example, if the customer is having some problems with your invoicing process, he may fixate on the problem in such a way that it prevents him from seeing a different solution. He may be complaining that his paper invoice is too slow in getting to him. The solution may not be in re-working the paper invoicing, mailing, or internal handling processes at all, but rather may be in moving to electronic invoicing and facilitating a three-way, on-line match. Or maybe the solution should be to eliminate the invoice entirely and re-work the payment process.

We need to understand the world from your customer's view of the world. There can be many forums for collecting Voice of Customer (VoC) information. My favorite is to do a "road show" and get onto the customer's turf. Then they can pull in the right expertise if they have questions about how changes may impact their business process.

A broader audience at the customer's site can also help others gain a full understanding of what you are trying to accomplish. Other times you will get little information during the VoC activity itself, yet gain valuable learning. We were conducting videotape interviews of a web order management application. The intention was to learn how intuitive our site was by turning the user loose to place an order, without giving him either training or printed instructions. After all, web pages don't always say what we expect them to say. The only instructions were on-line and they were very minimal.

The user needed to rely on the names of the buttons on the web page to navigate through the application. We asked the users to "chat away" as they did things on the screens to know what they were thinking and especially what questions came to mind. If users had questions, even if they successfully made it through the labyrinth, we would spot the difficulties and make changes to the wording on the screen.

Usually this worked very well. But one time the customer was going from screen to screen, entering data (correctly) and not saying a word the whole time. We kept prompting him to comment, but he remained silent. He was concentrating so hard, he didn't hear us, I guess. When he successfully had completed all the tasks, he only had one comment: "Now don't screw it up." That was a message we hadn't considered and we recognized the need to repress the impulse to monkey with things too much.

One customer told me he wanted to take out some price, but "not that much price." That was surprising as I had always been warned that in that channel, the dealers would extract blood until we were extinct, if we let them. But he explained to me that competition was a good thing because it drove price down and service up. But when there was no profit to be had, competitors would begin dropping out of the game. When there was only one supplier remaining, he would then be at the mercy of that supplier. He didn't care as much about winning the battle as he did about winning the war.

I like to document our "understanding" by writing customer scenarios. Another way of handling this is to incorporate this material in your application functional use case. These can then be confirmed with the customer to make sure you have captured the key points and have found any "stop signs." This allows for a mutual understanding of the design and also helps the customer see that his VoC contribution has not been in vain. It doesn't mean that this will be the final design, as you will want to collect input from a variety of sources and you also may have technical roadblocks or inaccurate data with which to contend. It just means, at that point in time, this was your vision.

It is the basis upon which trust is built. Walking in the other guy's shoes leads to greater understanding, compassion, and commitment. You have to ask yourself: What does it mean to walk in the other guy's shoes?

There is great value in just listening, just having your trading partner explain his hopes, issues, and concerns. There is also great value in creating and maintaining user councils, to get the same group of people together to talk through processing and problems. I ran a user council that talked through supply chain issues and packaging problems. Over time these led to entirely different packaging for a major line of products and enhanced bar coding. This made the products move more quickly and smoothly through the supply chain and far easier to identify on the retailer's shelf.

Often user councils are created for the wrong reason, however. This user council, which was so successful in revamping packaging, was created for absolutely the wrong reason. It was created to deliver a message to the dealers that to reduce cost we were eliminating some warehouses. User councils are not for lectures and one-way messages. User councils are for coming together and improving understanding.

People want to help. People want you to value their input. They want to be consulted and to participate in user councils, pilots, and prototypes. They don't always have the time to participate, so you may need to figure out different ways they can. Maybe you just offer to keep them abreast of what you discover from other users' input. Maybe you can offer to give them a quick call once a month to "touch base" and keep them posted on developments. In any event, be judicious in what you ask them to do. It needs to be more of a hobby for them than a full time job.

This regularly managed process, when consistently done, demonstrates trust to your trading partner. Over time, you can move far beyond where you have been in your customer relationships. The opposite is also true. If you don't follow through, don't communicate, or don't behave according to what you have discussed, there is no longer a reason to trust you. They will, however, understand when things are out of your control. Communication is the key. It also works to take away the fears we have of one another.

Users are smart people. You want to reward those who commit the time and energy to pass along their experience to you. They can also understand how to put the puzzle together differently-- in ways you haven't seen. Some of these will not be appropriate and will not "pan out." Others will only give you a kernel of what you need. Your trading partners can be rich assets, which you will want to tap frequently for mutual benefit.

It tells us how we are to negotiate. This is not figuring out how to take advantage of a situation. This is figuring out how you and your trading partner can together take best advantage. We then know what value the customer places on certain things and we have part of the equation complete. We then need to determine, within the confines of what the customer values, what value we can extract.

Buyers frequently want to receive invoices electronically. It helps facilitate their matching of the invoice to the purchase order. Sellers frequently want electronic payment. It reduces complexity, handling, and DSO. Knowing what you want and what your trading partner wants allows you to "bundle" your offering: Giving something to get something.

Walking in the other guy's shoes is a journey. But we still have to walk. The next time we go down the same (or a similar) path, we can see the world from two viewpoints, not just one.

When we walk in the other guy's shoes, we see the world from his viewpoint and we experience life in a different way. It opens our minds to different possibilities. It allows us to apply new and different methods and examples of how others have been successful.

Example is the school of mankind, and they will learn at no other.

Edmund Burke (1729-1797)

Practice Makes Perfect

I guess I was the typical boy in kindergarten. I was lazy and there was nothing that couldn't distract me.

Miss Waters gave each of us "dittos" on which to draw. In those days the copier was still a long way from being introduced into the schoolhouse. These copies, which came out of some long forgotten, God-forsaken copying process, smelled funny and produced purple lines on a sheet of white paper. Really they were just outlines of pictures. They would have things on them like a boy wearing a striped shirt and swinging a baseball bat with a dog running alongside.

I took my sheet of paper and scribbled on it with blue crayon. I ran the crayon cross the page as fast and as furiously as I could. When the page was mostly all blue, I admired my work and went on to some distraction.

Scribbling did serve a purpose. We learned to hold a pencil from holding crayons. We wrapped our fingers around it in the same way. We rested it between our thumbs and index fingers in the same way. We learned not to put too much pressure on the crayon to assure that it would not break, and later we did the same with our pencils. When we transitioned to pencils, we had tried out many of the skills already.

But Miss Waters said to me, "Don't you want to color a pretty picture?"

What? Was she talking to me? Was she implying this wasn't a pretty picture? What was wrong with her? It obviously was some kid playing baseball and it was Dodger blue. What could be prettier than that? What could be more "baseball" than that?

She explained that it would be better if the dog weren't blue and the bat weren't blue and the grass weren't blue. That if I colored each item in the picture with its appropriate color, the scene would be more realistic and more beautiful.

Okay. I could see her point. She gave me a second sheet and I scribbled each item on the page with its appropriate color. I would rummage through the cigar box of crayons and select one that I liked. I ran the crayon cross each item as fast and as furiously as I could. This was a bit harder, but it was fun selecting an interesting color.

When the page was nearly done, I admired my work. I was thinking to myself the dog is black, the bat is brown, and the grass is green. Perfect. Has there ever been any more realistic and beautiful ditto? It is time to go on to another distraction.

But Miss Waters handed me a third ditto and said, "Now try staying within the lines." She pointed out how, when I colored the stripes on the shirt for example, the orange color got on the boy's arms and face and grass.

Okay. I could see her point. I tried it. Hey, it was hard work. It took physical skills, dexterity, and determination to learn to color between the lines. It also took a great deal of concentration (and I didn't have much to spare). Most of all, it took a lot of practice.

We don't think of it as such, but coloring between the lines was a skill we had to learn. It was bringing multiple abilities together to do something new. Like anything we need to learn or seek to do, it starts with determination.

You have to "want it." This is the starting point of any eBusiness program. This goes far beyond the lip service we hear at so many companies. This is not management pontificating the eBusiness "phrase of the day." This is not pacifying someone's performance expectations that your company have some eBusiness project.

In B2B, it is not a matter of having options; it is a matter of which options to pick. It is making a conscious decision concerning what to develop and what to implement. You have to determine "why" you need to do something, not just what to do. It is in discovering why you are desperate for B2B that you sow the seeds of success.

In a company I worked with, we identified more than 200 projects in eBusiness when we surveyed activities around the globe. In a world where we want to foster entrepreneurship and experimentation, this may not sound bad. However, these are non-connected, disparate efforts that bleed away resources and don't leverage our learning. It is hard enough to marshal the right talent and abilities, but doing so without some corporate-wide benefit was throwing away money.

We hadn't asked ourselves the foundational questions that we needed to know for each project: "Why do we want this?" and "What are the business benefits these projects will derive?" and "What were the root causes that need to be ferreted out, instead of doing these specific projects?"

To be more than just marginally successful with B2B, you have to want it so badly you can taste it. They say that the best reengineering projects are those focused on the nearly hopeless causes. There is a similar truth to that with B2B.

You need to know who you are and what you are about. eBusiness is table stakes. Using eBusiness to take out cost is not.

However, typically, managers believe eBusiness is mostly about taking out cost. They may say otherwise, but the conversation always draws back to cost. In fact, eBusiness is about "faster, better, cheaper." My experience has been that if you go after "faster and better," reduced cost will take care of itself. Usually, far more cost is taken out than if you go after "cheaper" as the principle objective.

It is not surprising that most companies try to use B2B to cut cost. But unless your culture is driven by operational excellence, these efforts will only be marginally successful. You may also cut your own throat by giving a conflicting corporate message.

If your company is a product leader, be a product leader with B2B.

If you are a customer-intimate company, use B2B to be customer-intimate.

If your company's focus is on operational excellence, so be it. By definition, you have to be the low-cost model. Work on return on investment, nearly (but not quite) at the exclusion of product and customer focus.

Our corporate mindsets prevent us from viewing the world from other angles. This contradiction plays out in front of our customers' eyes in B2B. Don't try to make yourself, or your company, something you are not. It brings to mind the adage about not trying to teach a pig to sing; it doesn't sound good and it aggravates the pig.

My company is paranoid (it's okay; most companies are). Some days we think of ourselves as product leaders and talk about the price premium our products can command. Then we turn around and drive out research and development that would have kept us as a product leader. The next day we pat ourselves on the back on the costs we have driven out and make no correlation to the market share we are losing. This also prevents us from presenting a crisp message to the marketplace.

You also need to know your position in the world. You need to understand your competition and where they are situated in their B2B developments. Use that understanding to define what you will be and how you will position yourself.

It takes perseverance and determination. B2B projects can be hair-raising. There will be setbacks. Count on it. There will be things you hadn't considered. Don't worry about it. Your assumptions and estimates will be wrong. Deal with it.

What gets you through these difficult times?

❑ Remembering that you still "want it so bad you can taste it."

❑ Remembering how desperately your company needs this.

❑ Remembering how you can knock your market on its ear.

❑ Remembering you are bigger than the problems before you.

You need to focus, not fidget. Concentrate on the task at hand. Set the dates of your project today. Take no excuses, from yourself or others, concerning why the dates cannot be met. Having said that, you also need to balance this with a realistic view of what can be accomplished during any particular phase. When in doubt, cut it down. Divide, divide, and divide. Break projects that cannot be completed in 120 days into small, deliverable chunks of functionality. Maybe your first project is just to investigate something you don't know. Maybe your first project is to get the right management commitment.

Plan for a series of projects. Plan to re-do a good portion of your work.

Practice Makes Perfect. Think in terms of many short-term projects. Then think of these projects as "warm-ups" to what you really want to accomplish. They are practice sessions for what you want to be. These should be 90 to 120 day projects from start to finish. Don't worry about whether the functionality you are going to deliver is too small. It is. You can deal with it in the next project, if it is relevant at that point. You may not, because you may have learned something different than you had expected with your first project.

Don't over-design, spending so much time getting everything so perfectly laid out on paper that you shorten development time. Time-box and "crunch" your design. Get the essentials covered, but don't kill off your project before the design gets passed over to the programmers. Use an interactive process between the designers and programmers to work out voids in your design.

Take your first project and do something small. Learn from it. Take your next project and build upon what you have done and what you have learned.

My father used to say "Do something, even if it's wrong." Practice is about doing something. Do what you think is right, and when it isn't, don't fret-- learn from it. My boss once wrote to me, "You delivered exactly what the business units asked for and they immediately wanted to change it. How did that make you feel?" I wrote back, "Par for the course."

Patiently accept the fact that you will have to do everything multiple times for two reasons: first, to clean up what functionality you may have missed and, second, to keep your web site fresh.

I never think of B2B functionality as being "done." It is always in the process of getting to where I want it to be.

Just keep practicing and keep getting better.

Practice is the best of all instructors.

Publius Syrus (42 B.C.)

Expect Change

I don't remember what her name was. All I knew was that she wasn't Miss Waters. I was sure she was nice and would take good care of us. But she was ancient. She was closer to my grandmother's age than Miss Waters'. She wore a flowered dress and sat at the front of the classroom near the blackboard. I remember that she frequently read to us. She explained that Miss Waters was taking care of some urgent school business and that she would be with us for a while instead. I didn't know the school had a business. I am not sure I liked this change. Miss Waters had been with us every other day.

There were always other ladies in the room helping out. They were nice and helpful and just seemed to know what to do without anybody asking.

When this other lady was in our classroom, things didn't go as smoothly. Her helpers had to ask what she wanted them to do next. She didn't seem very sure of herself. We followed the same schedule, like going to recess at the same time, but things just seemed to be different. Kindergarten was just a little wrong somehow.

We live in a world that is continually changing. We don't always acknowledge that, but it is true. We like to lock into the things that are comfortable. Like wearing the same sweatshirt when we relax, there are certain patterns we just seem to enjoy. I guess we are all creatures of habit.

I find that even when I am doing something new, I follow the same old patterns. I think through the sequence of how things will work in the same way. I map out my work and personal activities in the same way. I probably even hit the old blind spots in the same way. That is, of course, if I have any blind spots! Life could be fine and comfortable, if "they" would just leave us alone.

But in eBusiness, we need to think in terms of morphing the business model continually. That doesn't mean we always throw out the old and move on to the new (though there is a place for that). It means that we have to continually look at the value equation and see what should change for ourselves and for our trading partners.

Change is necessary. We don't play all the cards. Things will change around us as we find better ways of doing things, create other processes or establish new relationships. As humans we are driven to build the better mousetrap and sometimes we get snapped.

There can be competitive changes, such as moving from analog to digital technologies. We wouldn't have experienced sustained technological change over the last forty-five years if we didn't actively seek out change. Think of the semiconductor industry that has doubled capacity on the computer chip every eighteen months or less. Companies that compete in those industries either leap frog the competition or are hanging on just to stay in the game.

There are market changes, where consumer preferences swing from one place to another. This is exemplified in the fashion industry, where sometimes even old styles return to the scene and the market adjusts. They change and change and they change back.

There are changes in the environment and corresponding regulatory agencies and public opinion changes, which dramatically impact markets.

The point is that we control none of this ourselves. Get used to it. The worse thing to do is to resist it.

In the eBusiness world, it can happen so quickly that we see changes in direction before some technologies are even deployed. In B2B exchanges, for example, a short time ago everyone was moving to public exchanges. As companies considered the risk and reward, they switched gears and moved to private exchanges instead. Public exchanges (temporarily) have become irrelevant.

Don't change for the sake of change. Baseball teams do this all the time. Mostly it doesn't work. Sometimes it makes us feel better that we are doing something creative or at least responding in some way. Change, for the sake of change, typically introduces new risks into the equation. Change is necessary, but not all change is necessary.

When we change things we can make our customers and suppliers uncomfortable. We can force them to buy and use new tools. We can force them to learn new things and hire more people. We can even force them to look elsewhere for their business opportunities and create other undesirable responses.

We need to carefully assess the impact that any change will make-- even a good change. There can be very minor changes, such as changing the banner on a web page that are neutral changes. And there can be other, seemingly minor changes that have unforeseen impacts. Our banner included the World Trade Center pictured prominently in the background. After the terrorist attack, would we keep the banner to honor those who were lost? Would we remove the view so that our customers and we were not continually reminded of our pain? Eventually we would have to change the banner, but what was the right timing?

Some change just isn't worth it. Make sure the emotional investment you may be asking others to make is worthwhile.

Change is frequently difficult. We all need to be reminded that change frequently is difficult. Not always, but frequently. If we don't remind ourselves of that fact, we don't look it straight in the eye. We don't understand the magnitude of the emotional and mental task before us. We sugar coat the tough decisions that will need to be made. We don't give them the due consideration and look at all the impacts.

At a company I worked for, change management is always at the forefront. I don't necessarily think that we always do a great job with change management, but its impact is always considered and work is done to mitigate or control risk. But you can't think of everything, so you can't mitigate every risk. Our brains don't work that way.

Recognizing change focuses our attention on the need for training and job aids. It can help us define new skills that are needed. It can help us work through the social aspects of work and job displacement.

One project I was on had outstanding savings and would have reduced customer service agents by a very dramatic number. But we also understood that our supply chain needed major attention. We could have eliminated all those jobs and not had the resources to work on the supply chain issues. But understanding the changes we were going through allowed us to recognize that the skills for our next most immediate issue were readily available. By moving some people, instead of eliminating more jobs, we were able to get to our end state objective quickly.

Don't worry about things you cannot control. There are many changes with which we have to deal over which we at least some degree of control. There are other things where we have no control (like the weather) or no longer have much control (like my teenage son). It doesn't do a bit of good to worry about things we cannot influence or control. Think, then, in terms of how you can respond to changes around you. How you respond includes how nervous, excited, or distracted you will get.

The key is to not get overly concerned with the change; instead, work your way to defining your path forward.

We gain some control in "controlling" change. We cannot always control circumstances. But we can gain control over some aspects of change. For example, we have influence over our emotions. Sometimes we can buck ourselves up to get ready for change. Sometimes we can talk to others who have experienced similar types of change and can help us through the process.

We can also sometimes modify the timing of change. This is not stalling, which is our typical approach when confronted with change. Many times people will attempt to wait things out, to see if the change will stick. This is typically not the best approach. We can always take responsibility in being prepared for a change.

The great dichotomy of B2B is that we cause change on an audience that doesn't want to change. All the technology aspects are easy by comparison. All the great technological advances are meaningless until everyone is ready to implement.

Just like with my substitute teacher, some changes are unavoidable no matter how much we may dislike them. But we can keep a sharp focus on how the change will impact others. I am sure my substitute teach was doing all in her power to make the transition on the kids as smooth as possible. We need to do likewise.

To be successful with B2B, you don't demand change by others; you teach, you illustrate, you negotiate, you gain consensus, you develop, you monitor, you adjust, you accomplish, you measure, and you celebrate. Then you take a deep breath and start the cycle all over again, until you get the job done right.

Welcome to my world!

"It is not necessary to change. Survival is not mandatory."

W. Edwards Deming

If at First You Don't Succeed, Try, Try Again

I remember the local electric company came to school each year to talk about safety around electrical wires. Southern California Edison would make their presentation, provide a safety cartoon booklet (who can forget "Sparky?"), and hand out kits containing materials for making kites. Their timing was perfect, because it always seemed to be windy the day they presented. They would encourage us to think about safety when using kites and to involve our parents in kite-construction.

In hindsight, that was pretty remarkable. Today I cannot imagine a power utility company risking the liability of teaching kids to make a toy that, if misused, could result in injury or death. Obviously our world has changed a bit. In those bygone days, maybe they recognized that I was going to fly a kite whether they taught me the safe way to do so or not. Maybe they were a lot smarter then, smarter than their lawyers are today.

My father helped me make that first "electric company" kite. He also helped me make a kite he always enjoyed flying-- a "box kite" made out of newspaper, string, and pieces of wood. I have loved box kites ever since. They took hours to make and great care was necessary to get the strings in place and the frame square. We worked together gluing the paper and creating notches in the wood for the string.

It was a masterpiece.

He told me to hold the kite while he walked, then ran. He had instructed me to let go of the kite when he yelled. I watched him run. I watched the string tighten. I was admiring the way the kite was capturing the wind when he called for me to let go. Then I watched a piece of the wood snap because I had held on to the kite too long. I watched as he stormed back into our house, disappointed in me.

The next day I apologized to my father. Soon we fixed the box kite and got it soaring in the wind.

We all make mistakes. We all miscalculate and make wrong assumptions. We also observe others (and sometimes maybe ourselves) intentionally or unintentionally blind ourselves to realities we don't choose to admit. It is no different in the business world or in our personal lives.

With eBusiness, it just seems that the other guy's calculation of benefits doesn't quite mirror our own vision of reality or our experience.

One other thing that is typically different about eBusiness is that we rely on others for our own success. That introduces an additional dynamic in achieving, or failing to achieve, success. That potential trading partner with whom you have been working for months and who has been solidly behind your project "all the way", suddenly has his funding evaporate. Or it is technically more difficult than they had thought and they cannot bring the right resources to bear to complete the project. Or their "security people" will not let them pass through your firewall in the way they thought they could. Or whatever.

With eBusiness, this reversal of fortune can happen very quickly.

A third problem with eBusiness is the way we approach our projects. Our inclination is to turn our pilots and prototypes into full-fledged, production applications. Shame on us. A proof of concept is getting the kite ten feet off the ground for ten seconds, not to a hundred feet for an hour. This is the place we make our "break throughs" with customers-- in their thinking and commitment. This is where we prove to management, our trading partners, and, yes, to ourselves as well, that our plans can be made to work.

We need to understand what we expect to learn and ideally determine how we are going to measure our pilots and prototypes. We need to do that first.

Our inclination is to place too much into the "first release." We aim too high with functionality, performance, scale implementations, etc. Shame on us again.

In reality, if something cannot be completed in a 60-to-90 day cycle, it is already too big. Break it down. If it still seems to be too big, it is. The next step is easy! Your first 30-day project is to figure out how you are going to break all your work down into 60-to-90 day projects.

One of my colleagues did a great job breaking down projects into "bite-size chunks" without compromising the design. She recognized the value of getting "something done" while moving the much larger project along. She stayed focused on the final objective and made sure there was alignment to the short-term objective. She continually kept the features that were taken "off the plate" for the current development visible so that, at the appropriate time, it could be reincorporated. Many times this last step is lost. We take out functions or feature in our effort to meet a schedule without understanding how it compromises the overall design. Then it is all too easy to ignore what has been "dropped out" when we move along to the next project. It can also be the Trojan horse in B2B. It can mean the different between failure and success that we neglect to recognize until it is too late.

Anything bigger than a 60-to-90 day project is too dynamic to create at all, much less create well. The problem is that this runs counter to the way we as business people are configured. We are so anxious to get big things going, we don't recognize when our earnest endeavor is leading down a blind alley.

Fail fast and fail small. Failure is natural. Unfortunately, we are not conditioned for failure. We don't hold commencement ceremonies for those who flunk out of school. (Maybe we should. Actually, they are just commencing early and moving on to their next educational experience.) Instead, we take failure personally. We never plan for it. Our plans call for us to mitigate our risks instead of planning for what we hope to extract out of a failure.

Haven't we all seen organizations struggle just to get started with a project that seems too big? We all have seen projects that seems as if they spent all their time trying to gain traction, not knowing exactly where to begin.

Have you ever read a business case that said, "We don't know enough to be successful, so we plan on this being a complete write off and will be coming back for more money to do it again soon?" I don't think so. We would be handed our hat, if not our head! But in reality that is where we frequently find ourselves in B2B, especially if we have done a good job with our business and eBusiness strategies. Especially if our plans have stretched our imaginations.

The paradigm we need to move to is one that the best research organizations hit upon: "One of these will work, we are just not sure which one yet!"

Instead of being overly concerned with failure, you want to control failure and learn from it. Extract as much learning as possible from things that don't work. Find out why the acceptance of your application has been less than stellar. Failing small and failing fast go "hand in hand." They enable us to pick ourselves up off the mat and get back into the game.

When I worked for Kodak, our business units and customers told us that we needed to have order status and carrier tracking. They told us order status was far more important than order entry. We knew that order entry was still important, since our corporate management was driving us hard to take out costs. So we developed both web-based functions.

Our initial experience, however, was that order entry was used far more by customers than order status. Since this is contrary to what we had been told by the business units and key customer contacts would happen, we looked at the process to determine why. We found that as customers did order entry, we were supplying the information that was most important to them both on-line and via a separate e-mail. We were giving them the estimated delivery date for each item. If there were going to be multiple shipments of an item, each delivery quantity and its correlating delivery date was identified. Because of this information, much of the need for order status was taken away. Customers only needed to come to order status to confirm that items were still on schedule or to follow-up should we have late deliveries.

This means our needs assessment failed. But it doesn't mean we hadn't done a good job with the needs assessment. Nobody could have told us ahead of time what would have occurred. Customers were being shown order entry and order status at the same time, yet they didn't catch how their behaviors would have been different. Nobody was jumping up and down saying, "Why don't you give us just order entry instead?" Their most recent experience with the manual processes had driven them to have in mind one solution, when another solution was better suited for their needs.

Would that have changed the functionality that we would have delivered? Possibly. We might have developed order status in smaller segments of work and accessed each one differently. It certainly would have changed our customer rollout process.

Learn to throw the first waffles out. You learn by doing. Confucius said, "I hear and I forget. I see and I remember. I do and I understand." We can all relate.

You can get all the consulting you want. You can attend all the classes. You can listen to all the lectures. You can attend all the seminars. You can watch over the shoulders of others. But there is nothing like doing it yourself. It's where the rubber meets the road. It is where you begin to understand. There is nothing like getting your hands on the steering wheel.

I occasionally have the opportunity to help a business unit define its eBusiness strategy. In reality I am not sure there is such a thing as an eBusiness strategy, but most people don't know that early on. There should be a business strategy and the eBusiness components need to support and align with that overarching strategy.

I use a methodology called a "strategy table" to help bring clarity to the effort. The first three steps can be done in either workshops or as preparation work leading up to a workshop. The initial steps lead the business unit leadership through understanding the scope, marketplace, and competition.

The idea is, in a progressive fashion, to most narrowly focus the effort and to do so quickly. With pinpoint precision, we try to decide what the eBusiness effort will and will not entail. That way, the workshop participants have some management direction and basis upon which to proceed. Without that direction, participants can wander in the wilderness for 40 years!

It never ceases to amaze me how businesses hit a "wall of discovery" at about this point. Usually, they have clearly misjudged the opportunity and need to regroup. Or they have misalignment with their business unit or corporate goals. Or they have singled out the effort for a small group (or individual) that hasn't fully represented their senior management's most crisp thinkers.

Almost always, some additional effort is required as a "course correction." It doesn't matter how often ahead of time I have preached gaining senior management participation.

I always give warnings from my previous experience, but until the participants arrive at the "do" stage, it just doesn't click. They will nod their heads in philosophical agreement with the warnings and inveritably proceed down the path until they hit that same wall of discovery. Finally it clicks.

No longer do I get red in the face. I don't jump up and down any more. No longer do I get angry when they have proceeded through my warning. I have learned to throw out the waffles.

You know how it is when you cook waffles: you use the first batch to season the grill. You get everything to the right temperature. The first batch is always undercooked or overcooked or both at the same time. It's not fit to eat. You might drool a little, but you toss them to the dog and get on to the next batch.

It is the same thing with creating an eBusiness strategy and with executing that first strategy. Even if you have a good strategy, you are not going to get the execution step right. Get over it and get on with its replacement.

I recommend that eBusiness strategies be "refreshed" every six months. Get all the workshop participants, senior management, and interest holders together for a day to assess where you have been and to make appropriate changes. Usually, these will be only small changes.

But have the courage to throw out a flawed strategy; it's just a waffle.

Understand the consequences of any failure. If your job is on the line, it isn't a pilot. Everyone needs to clearly understand expectations for both success and failure. It is best to get on paper what the key points of failure will be and how you intend to mitigate those risks. At some point, there will be just too many unknowns or a series of uncertainties mounded on top of one another to reasonably calculate an outcome. At that point, you cannot just throw up your hands. It is best at this stage to review your dilemma with management and get it all out in the open. Once it is, your task is to make sure it transitions from being "in the open" to "on paper."

This is not essentially a "cover your tail" exercise; it is also an avenue to circulate the problem to a wider audience who may have had a similar experience or may know of other ways to manage the risk.

Take the edge off failure by keeping the risk down.

It's an itsy bitsy spider world. There is a great deal to be learned from the song we teach our children:

The Itsy-bitsy spider went up the waterspout,

Down came the rain and washed the spider out.

Out came the sun and dried up all the rain,

So the itsy-bitsy spider went up the spout again.

It's not the end of the world if you fail, provided you have set the right expectations. It's just the end of this round, and now it's time to go on to the next round. Buck yourself up. Remain enthusiastic. Don't allow yourself or others to get discouraged. Take courage. Continue to trust your intuition. Keep trying. You'll get it right.

Some day your kite will soar.

'Tis a lesson you should heed, Try, try again. If at first you don't succeed, Try, try again.

Thomas H. Palmer (1782 - 1861) Teacher's Manual (1840)

Milk and Cookies

Do you remember the celebrations we had in kindergarten?

We would all participate and enjoy the celebration. If it was your birthday, you were really someone special that day! You would get to sit in the "birthday chair" at the front of the class near the teacher. We would all wear birthday hats and sing "Happy Birthday" to the celebrity of the day.

Any event in our lives seemed worthy of a celebration. After all, it wasn't just birthdays that were our special events. Special events were Grandmother coming for a visit or a cat having kittens. It was the first day of spring or a new baby brother.

For these extra special celebrations, cupcakes with swirled frosting washed down with orange Kool-Aid™ were a special treat! I can taste them right now. Can you? That wasn't too much sugar for you, was it?

Miss Waters would announce the big success or the happy event. She would explain why it was important. Which sometimes wasn't all that obvious. It didn't need to be important to everyone; it just needed to be important to one person. She might explain that Marbee's grandmother was "out from Chicago" for her grandson's Bar Mitzvah. Our teacher would explain why that was significant to Marbee, her brother, and her grandmother. Then she would ask Marbee about her grandmother and what special memories they shared. She was building for Marbee something for which to be thankful. She was celebrating her family. She was also building for her a desire to do well and to make her family proud.

The room mother would organize some of the celebrations. Mothers would do the shopping and baking and make special trips to school to hand out the goodies. It was always fun when your mom came to class.

With our faces covered in frosting and sticky hands all around, our mothers and Miss Waters would share in the special moment.

There were rewards for small successes in the classroom, like a good job sharing or bringing back Marvin's cage exceptionally clean (Marvin was our guinea pig). The celebration didn't need to be elaborate to be meaningful. For those smaller celebrations it was typically "milk and cookies." Seemed like we had a little celebration almost every day. Milk and cookies were just fine with me. Each of us would be instilled with the encouragement to do well and the desire to please.

Over time the rewards for achievement became fewer and fewer. By the time we entered high school the acknowledgments had become typically negative punishments instead of positive reinforcements. After two solid weeks of diligent study to get through midterms and "finals," with the threat of not making it into the college of our choice, we were left emotionally and mentally exhausted. Our positive reward was sometimes just our own momentary sigh of relief as we hunkered down to begin the next semester.

When we entered the business world, this translated into arcane annual performance reviews. You know the process. We start the year by guessing what we can do. There are really too many dynamics and too many things that are out of our control that influence this process to make those guesses realistic. But we have to get something on paper, so we call these our "personal goals." We are handed "team goals" over which we have less or even no control. Taken together, those become our "performance expectations."

We write these expectations down, file away that paper, and, in the hectic pace of getting our "real" work done, we forget about it, until we periodically meet with our boss to see what progress we have made. We attempt to convince him to make adjustments to align with how the real world is turning. Yet the boss looks at those adjustments with dollar signs in his eyes. He sees those adjustments as a "risk" for higher wages and bigger bonuses than the budget will allow. It doesn't fit into his neat little world. It doesn't matter what the goal <u>really</u> should be.

Then at the end of the year we compare the "performance expectations" against our perceived results. It all seems such a waste of time and so irrelevant.

In normal business the pace of change is fast enough, but in the eBusiness world we live at a frantic pace. Our performance reviews seem even more irrelevant and even harmful to the progress we need to make.

If we can really drive to multiple, overlapping eBusiness projects, both our traditional measuring process and rewards need to go out the window. There is plenty of opportunity to celebrate. But we need performance rewards that mirror the rapid nature, intensity, and level of commitment of B2B. Someday our companies may get there; until then, we need to look more introspectively.

Reflect on your week each week. I try to set aside a few minutes each week to reflect on what we have done. Just a few minutes on Friday, alone in my office, reviewing my calendar for the week just completed and looking forward into the following week.

It is not easy and I often find myself slipping into how much is left to be done, rather than recognize how much has been accomplished. With eBusiness projects we have an opportunity to break the work down into small, meaningful cycles. As we get better with that we need to remain mindful of how much is being accomplished. We need to establish communications techniques and forums for making others aware of both our trials and accomplishments.

I recently gave a talk that reflected on all that we had accomplished over the past two years. Whew! It was amazing how much we had done. If I hadn't been asked to talk on that specific subject, I wouldn't have gone back and looked at the facts and figures. Oh, I knew them in pieces; I had quoted them often enough. But I didn't reflect on the whole picture. I wouldn't have made all the comparisons that were relevant. I have enough to do in the present to not worry about the past.

It had slipped up on us that, in ten months, we had grown our volumes ten fold and had another ten fold increase in user volume expected over the next five months! But more importantly we had taken for granted all that we had learned and all the challenges we had overcome. We knew a great deal more now about what we needed to do to be successful, but we hadn't shared that with others. We hadn't made their lives easier. We hadn't encouraged those struggling with the same issues and climbing up the same learning curve. We had left others to reinvent the wheel. We had looked at this as "tooting our own horn." We should have looked at it as giving others a hand. In reality, we should be expected by others to do both.

Celebrating your successes. In kindergarten it was "kittens and coloring;" now it is quality review boards and "phases and gates" reviews. Now it is management presentations and business cases. The world has changed a bit around us.

Sometimes we have had bosses who were real mentors. They knew what to say and when. They were more encouragers than taskmasters.

Over time I have seen fewer and fewer of those types of bosses. I have an unproven theory that this all changed when layoffs became pervasive across the business landscape. Now bosses have a conflict. An encouragement and high praise could seem contradictory to the judge, when the highly arbitrary employee ranking process places that highly praised individual in the lower quadrant!

We have lost something. We have lost someone to remind us of our accomplishments on a frequent basis. We have lost someone to remind us that there is a time to have our heads down in the details and a time to hold our heads up high. Certainly they remind us enough to keep our noses to the grindstone.

If you are managing an eBusiness operation you need to keep recognition on the forefront. You need to look for incremental steps to celebrate. This is not large scale, significant, costly celebrations (though there is a place for that). This is celebrating, recognizing, and rewarding our small steps and our large steps.

Celebrate others' successes. We need to take the time to congratulate others on their success. One of my prized memories is a note I received from a competitor. It said what a wonderful job I had done leading an initiative from which he and his company had benefited. While we were still competitors, he could see the value I had added to the community. He could also see how I had broken the ice with our mutual customers and how he could follow in my footsteps.

This is not, however, something I feel I do well. I feel awkward telling people what a nice job they have done, because I hate that pained look of embarrassment on another's face. One person I work with does a great job of saying "great job" frequently, sincerely, and unabashedly. I know I should and can do better.

Like most people I also get inwardly focused and need to make the commitment of time and energy to look more diligently around me.

Celebrate small successes. We need to celebrate our own successes. We cannot wait for that significant reward that comes every so often and frequently gets "hung up" based on business cycles, economic conditions, and budget squabbles.

Part of celebrating is renewing in us the desire to do well. Part of celebrating is remembering that work has its own rewards. I can despair at my company's financial performance, while at the same time recognizing my own contributions to our success "against the tide."

Nothing wrong with an extra dessert once in a while, is there? Nothing wrong with taking the family out to dinner and discussing your "mini-victory."

Cookies still work. Bon appetite!

Be satisfied with success in even the smallest matter, and think that even such a result is no trifle.

Marcus Aurelius (121-180)

Take a Nap in the Afternoon

Whether we were tired or not, each afternoon in kindergarten we took a nap. It wasn't optional. It wasn't that kindergarten was physically demanding. We would have recesses that allowed us to blow off "excess energy," so the day certainly didn't wear us out. My mother used to say that if she could bottle and sell that excess energy she would be a wealthy woman. Probably true.

Naptime wasn't about recovering our strength. It was about settling our spirits. It was about coming down to a level where we could pay attention, learn, and do our best. It seemed that after naptime we would have the most creative, most imaginative times of the day.

We pulled out small mats, which we laid on the floor. They were thin and hardly longer than our bodies. We didn't have pillows. We would lie down and try to be quiet. Miss Waters would pull the shades to darken the room a bit, but there was still plenty of light. I don't remember the teacher having to "get after us" about being quiet. I don't know that any of us ever slept, but maybe some of us did. Maybe the teacher slept. The teacher wouldn't speak to us except in whispers. She was setting an example of being quiet for us. We could still hear the street noises, traffic, construction, and workers talking far off in the background.

We would rest for just a short period of time. It probably wasn't more than ten minutes, but sometimes it seemed like an eternity. Often it was hard to remain still. But after we got used to naptime (and figured out there was no escaping it), we were able to settle down quickly and really rest. Afterward, we would hear a story or do some highly creative activity.

We have lost something during the span of my working life. At one time, everyone would take a lunch hour together and have a coffee break in the morning and afternoon. It was a social time. It was a time of being together and seeing each other in a different light. We would share a laugh together and relax. We would share our lives. We certainly would talk about work issues, but frequently in a different light. Unfortunately, we did not understand the value of this time, either as companies or as individuals.

As companies, we viewed this time as optional. Breaks were an interruption to the <u>real</u> work activity. That's when we expected the employee to take care of his/her personal business. If they didn't have any personal business that day, well, there was always plenty of <u>real</u> work to be done. In today's era of massive layoffs, it is a time where we can catch up on work, where the work that hadn't been driven out of the process can be completed by the employees who hadn't been driven out yet.

For employees, it is a time we can make a small sacrifice so as not to have to make a larger sacrifice. Sacrifice a few minutes here and a few there, eat lunch at your desk, keep moving, so when 6:30 P.M. rolls along we can hustle home to spend a few minutes with the kids before bedtime. Only we are too stressed and weary to do a good job at those personal connections. Our personal lives have become as frazzled as our professional lives. We have been in a downward spiral.

As a young manager, we used to do off-site planning activities. We'd set aside a few days in the year to "retreat." We worked hard and played hard at retreats. The different setting allowed us to more fully concentrate on our future. We have forgotten the value of doing this type of activity as well. It was viewed as a luxury and an unnecessary expense. An ever-tightening belt squeezed them out.

It was where we took a fresh look at our plans and the way we operated. It was where we could challenge the paradigms that had become ruts. It was where we would make complete, cohesive, and intelligent plans. Today, our accountants would much prefer us spending an additional $50,000 doing rework than spending $5,000 upfront to plan it right. Oh, they never say that; they just live it. So instead of doing it the right way, we plan as we go: "Let's take that road, it seems to be going west."

Reflect on what you have done while the project is underway. In the heat of the moment, it is difficult to keep things in the right perspective. When you have a need to allocate more resources to development, for example, it is hard to determine whether those resources will ultimately improve quality or make less testing necessary. Either might be true, but don't count on either. Don't shortcut a step based on an assumption that may not prove to be correct.

Set aside thought time to consider how things are progressing. But be careful about "pulling the trigger" too early. Your job is to bring up the issues, not to solve them yourself or "micro-manage." This is a slow, steady hand on the rudder making small, smooth adjustments.

You can use a public forum such as team meetings or governance councils to raise questions such as "What have we missed here?" But do so in a non-threatening way. And come up with those pointed questions ahead of time during your naptime.

Wind your projects down. The wrap-up activities that get shortchanged are clean up of the documentation, sharing experiences and learning from final testing and training, modification of the metrics to be applied against the application, and establishing robust production support activities.

The final stages of our projects need to have as many robust "gating" activities as the early stages. The early "gating" activities are always easy. We have to make sure that all aspects of the project have been put into place before we make substantial investment. In essence, we check out the "thoughtware" before we buy the hardware. Outside of out and out fraud, all companies have checks and balances to make sure there is some accountability before making a substantial investment. Thus they "gate" their future activities. "We have to have all of these things done before we will move on to those other things."

But as projects progress to their final stages of development, the desire to "get the project over with" begins to mount. We are anxious to see results. By the time we are ready for user acceptance testing, our emotional state (excitement) and mental stresses (exhaustion) are overpowering. We push and push to the goal line and to collapse.

We need to have as much rigor when the project is being completed as we had in starting the early phases. But to establish that rigor we need do two things.

First, we need to schedule adequate time at the end of projects for these activities. These cannot be shortchanged. This cannot be the place where we make-up for lost time during other phases of the project. At the start of the project, schedule adequate time for these activities. This is not "fat" in your schedule that can later be trimmed. It is adequate (not excess) time to do the job right. Then manage against that time and establish adequate measures for completion.

Second, we need to develop concrete management activities to monitor these final stages to make sure they remain on course. This is the hard work of management. The tendency is for management's attention to go elsewhere, like on starting the next wave of activities or the next fire drill. Nothing is more important to sustained success, however, than making sure we have done a good and complete job of what we have just completed. Nothing determines the scalability of a project like the close monitoring to make sure the final steps stay on track.

The quickest way to "age" a project is to not start with correct and cleaned up documentation. Getting that documentation "back in shape" is often a laborious and tedious proposition.

To make sure the documentation, such as job aids, meets the users' need, it is best to share experiences and learning from the final stages of a project, such as testing and training. This requires a major step back from the "hustle and bustle." This is another form of nap in the afternoon. In as relaxed an atmosphere as you can create, give everyone involved a chance to express their views. Find out what surprised them. Find out was displeased them. Listen to what was more difficult than they had expected. Don't be defensive about what they say. It is better to have to correct things now than after it is in the customer's hands. You may need to do some additional VoC work, to either confirm or rule out the concerns that are expressed. You may need to beef up some of the training materials, job aids, or help screens.

You may need to modify your metrics based upon what you hear. If there are concerns that lend themselves to measurement, try to put at least temporary measures in place. This is not the time to reduce expectations, but it is the time to refine your measurements.

Finally, you want to determine that your production support activities will be sufficiently robust. There is nothing worse than lack of support. Nothing will turn off a user base more or kill off an implementation more quickly. If a user calls the 800 number that you have given them and the person on the other end of the line "doesn't have a clue," it will reflect on your whole application.

But if you can anticipate those questions and document the answers (or at least identify who can answer them), you will be well on your way to robust production support. "Frequently asked questions" are not enough. That's reactive. You need to deliver, preemptively, another type of FAQ: "Fervently anticipated quips." These are answers to questions you think will come up or should come up--that you desperately want to answer. You are just hoping someone will ask the question so you can deliver the answer in the high way that it's importance be seen. The advantage you have is that you know the design "cold." You should be able to "see" what problems are likely to occur and what aspects may confuse a novice user. You can deliver the answer to those questions ahead of time--ahead of being asked.

You need to "dream" a good bit about what the user experience will be like, when the user has questions or concerns. You need to put yourself in their place: see the screens from their view and understand the thought process and information flow through which they are going.

Schedule some "down time" between your projects. We need to set aside time between projects to be introspective about what we have just completed. This is contrary to the way we normally schedule our activities. Generally, we jam one project right up against the next, even trying to get people pulled off the first project early in order to get a "jumpstart" on the next. This is foolish.

As a project leader, you may need to walk away from the project for a short time to get a real perspective of what is occurring and why. When either praise or criticism is pouring in, it is the time you are most vulnerable to bad judgment. You can overreact. It is your bad judgment that can have a major impact on your next project. It is time to rest and reflect.

It is time to settle your spirits. It is time to notch things back again.

Take pride in what you do and what you have accomplished. But also learn what you could have done better so you can apply it to what you will be doing next. This is not a good team activity. Raising questions and concerns immediately at the end of the project for many people can be counterproductive. You want to access, but not be overly critical. Ask, "What could be better next time?" as opposed to "What did we do wrong?"

It is time to "pull out the mat," reflect, and allow yourself to dream a bit.

As my mother used to say, "Sweet dreams."

"The brain is a wonderful organ; it starts working the moment you get up in the morning and does not stop until you get into the office."

Robert Frost

Measuring Progress

We didn't feel like we were being tested when we were in kindergarten. We didn't consider them "real tests" as we would later in grade school when we had rigorous examinations in math, social studies, and spelling. The tests we had in kindergarten were subtler. But, no doubt about it, every day we were being tested. Miss Waters was going through a continual evaluation of our abilities and measuring our progress in a wide range of areas.

Our ability to learn was being assessed. Our progress in building good work habits and group participation was being evaluated. Our self-control and discipline were being monitored. Our ability to pay attention was being watched. We were building some basic skills as a foundation upon which other skills would be developed.

I remember Miss Waters showing us flash cards with the letters of the alphabet. There was one letter on each card in bold, block font style with upper case on one side and lower case on the opposite side. We started learning the lower case letters. We would all "speak" each letter, as Miss Waters would flash them to us. Sometimes it was easy. Other times, we had to think about which letter she was showing us. She would go faster and faster each day. I had to really think whether she was showing us a lower case "b" or "d". I always yelled "O" when she showed us "Q." I was not the only one calling out the wrong letters. Over time it became easy. We weren't testing ourselves against the ability to read, we were testing ourselves against a smaller, foundational skill.

There were many reasons we were closely observed. (Other than the fact that half of us were boys!) She was continually asking herself, "What additional help was needed right now?" and "On which areas should his parents concentrate?" and "Can he be successful in first grade?" and "What will it take for him to be successful in life?"

These evaluations were necessary for our short-term success. Our short-term success was essential for long-term success.

The testing that takes place in kindergarten is different from other types of testing. It tested our readiness from a social standpoint to move on to more detailed and demanding types of work. Both our ability to concentrate and to absorb was assessed. Our mental, emotional, and social abilities were determined and a certain criteria had to be met before we were ready to move on. Only when we are ready should we move up to greater levels of work.

By our nature, we seem to want to move on to the "real work" in eBusiness. In the daily pressures to succeed, we press for the finish line without really doing all the tasks. Sometimes we get lucky and "skate" through a B2B implementation. When we do so, we are unable to duplicate our success. We falter the next time but are not sure why.

There are a few things that we willingly tend to give up in our quest: documentation and testing. Yet they play a key role in determining our likelihood for sustaining our programs.

Measure progress in order to adjust plans. We didn't receive the traditional "letter grades" in kindergarten: A, B, and C. Our grades were V, S, and N: Very Good Progress, Satisfactory, or Needs More Time. The grades and measures were appropriate to what we were expected to accomplish in the short-term.

Initially we were assessed against our ability to recognize letters. Once we had mastered that skill we would be assessed against our ability to identify sounds. With the previous skill mastered, the earlier measure was no longer necessary or advantageous. Progress against the next skill was now what was important. A new measure was needed.

If we faltered to sufficiently develop one of the "building block" skills, the teacher would adjust. We may have taken longer and concentrated more effort on the skill. Our parents would have been called on to help and given aids and instruction. The plans were based on need-- personal where needed and broad where appropriate.

The same thought should apply to our B2B projects.

Only measure if you are willing to take corrective measure. You need to assess real progress, not just "gate deliverables" or other artificial events. There is nothing worse than measuring the wrong thing or measuring for the wrong reason. This can demoralize a team and give them the wrong signal concerning what is important.

You should only set goals that you control. To be handed a goal by your boss is normal. To be handed a goal which seems unachievable is disheartening. But to be handed a goal where we cannot control or influence the outcome is ridiculous.

You have to think of our measures as you would a compass. You use a compass to make sure you are on the right path. When we have veered from the right path, we quickly know what to do about it.

You need to measure early and often. Monthly measures are generally best. But only measure if you are going to do something different if the measure "goes south." If you are going to sit on "pins and needles" just hoping things will turn around, the measures haven't done anything for you.

You will need to be able to "morph" the measure over time. Use the measure to know when you are ready for the next level. Move to the new goal and to a new measure. Progress is made in doing the two in tandem and not confusing which is which.

Start with knowing what you are ultimately going to measure. It is usually easier to think of the long-term goal, instead of the interim goals. That doesn't mean it is always easy to identify everything that you want to achieve.

Your goal may be 75% of your order entry transactions handled electronically. Sounds fair and reasonable. However, the goal might be better if it were "75% of your order entry transactions handled electronically while customer satisfaction is improved by 50%." The first goal might give you one time cost savings, but the combined goal gives you a sustainable solution that can be used elsewhere.

Your long-term goal needs to be framed in your customers' view of the world. Once you are happy with that goal, confirm it with a "Voice of Customer" (VoC) assessment. Your customer will tell you how they feel about the goals you propose. Next, work your way backward to establish interim and monthly goals. Just like with the reading "building blocks," one goal should lead to the next goal. One measure should lead to the next measure.

By doing this you set realistic goals, but also ones that can be exceeded. You know what exceeding the goal means. For example, if I set a goal to read one book this week and one book next week, I know how to exceed the first week's goal. I can begin to read the second book. I can get a "jumpstart" on the next week's goal. If I read the first book twice, I have done a great deal of addition work, but I haven't exceeded the goal.

Once you have established the goals, and know what it means to exceed the goals, you can go out and try to exceed them.

Measure-- even when it is hard. Sometimes it is nearly impossible or too expensive to set up quantitative measures. Instead, you may be able to use qualitative measures to get another view of the situation. People will generally have a good sense of whether progress is being made or not and frequently can come up with some alternate measure.

Test and measure to know you have succeeded. In kindergarten, reading was not required. But readiness to read was a key focus. Skills were being developed and evaluated in auditory and visual discrimination. If our measure had been on reading in kindergarten, we would have all failed. The step-by-step progress needed to be measured and monitored.

Once I was on a tirade about an inappropriate measure that a business unit was so proudly proclaiming. They were so exciting that they were moving the "needle," but failing to see that their measure was empty and meaningless in moving them along to achieving the long-term goal. I wrote a rhetorical question, "If they don't know where they are going, how are they going to get there?"

My colleague, Vince Bianchi, astutely summed it up in a few words, "Isn't that what Alice said?" It brought to mind a great truth from the conversation in Lewis Carrol's Alice in Wonderland: "Would you tell me, please, which way I ought to walk from here?" "That depends a good deal on where you want to get to," said the Cat.

"In this age, which believes that there is a short cut to everything, the greatest lesson to be learned is that the most difficult way is, in the long run, the easiest."

Henry Miller

Sometimes Things Go Wrong

I hated it when it rained at school. We would shift to "rainy day schedule." Whose idea was that? Afraid we were going to get wet and melt? Recesses were cancelled so we couldn't go outside to play. Though we played in the classroom, it just wasn't the same. It wasn't the physical release of energy that we all seemed to need. Not sufficiently rambunctious for my tastes.

One afternoon, in the middle of January, it began to hail. We lived near Los Angeles and hail there is rare. Some of the kids in our class had seen snow before and a few had experienced hail, but this was the first time I remember having seen such a thing. Someone explained to us that it was frozen rain. Amazing!

We became aware of the hail because of the noise. It no longer sounded like the strong rain we had been hearing during the last few days. It sounded like rock salt was being poured onto our roof and thrown onto the large windows. We had been sitting on the floor in the center of the classroom doing some quiet activity. When it began to hail, we just sat there looking at each other, not knowing what was happening. I don't recall the teacher saying anything to us. But in an explosion of excitement we all ran to the windows to see what was happening. It was a small stampede to the windows at the side of the room, where there were display tables and open storage bins, to see what was making all that noise. The hail was hitting the ground so hard it was literally bouncing a foot high! Some of the boys jumped onto the table to get a better view and knocked some things over. The hail looked like kernels of popcorn exploding everywhere. As quickly as the hail had come, it subsided. The noise turned from "salt" back to rain. Regaining control, Miss Waters began herding us back to the center of the classroom.

It was then that I noticed what appeared to be soapy water on the floor. And then I saw the broken plastic pieces. Reassembling the pieces together in my mind, I recognized what it was. I had brought a dome to class that day to share. I had received it as a Christmas present and was eager to show it off. It had been made of clear, white, and blue plastic and inside you could see the scene of a woodsman's cottage and a forest of tall pine trees. You turned the dome upside down and small plastic flakes fell into the top of the dome. When you righted the dome, it gave the appearance of snow slowly falling as the flakes descended through soapy water inside the dome.

If I had only given it to my teacher when class began, like my mom had told me. If only I had foreseen what could have happened.

Not noticing the damage (or the mess) Miss Waters announced it was time for "Show and Tell." Probably because I had been so excited about what I had to share, she called on me first. There I stood, having lost a Christmas present, with a mess on the floor, and nothing to share. I was heartbroken.

Things go wrong. That's part of life. We all know it. We all experience business disappointment. Actually, business is full of disappointments-- large and small. If you want a "wake-up call," take a look at the statistics on businesses that fail each year. Think how many of them were eBusinesses. The "death of the dot-coms" has almost become a modern day business lexicon for an imprudent, overly optimistic, failed, opportunistic investment (at its best) and greed, cupidity, and avarice (at its worst).

With eBusiness projects we have been pioneering in many ways. We have pioneered the technology and we have pioneered the finances. Many of us have worked through the first business cases on eBusiness projects at our companies. We have struggled and debated the benefits and ultimately accepted the challenges of "making it happen"--on both sides of the ledger.

We have engaged others in helping them to see our vision. We have accepted the helm of steering the ship through dangerous waters, when management waivered or gave it lip service, to what we knew in our hearts was the right course.

Frequently we make an emotional investment. The B2B projects become "our babies." I remember the day we received our first B2B web orders when I couldn't control my tears. My colleagues had spent the last few months of hard work to get the application all put together and tested, and they were thrilled to see it evolve. But for me it marked the culmination of six years' effort of taking it from "idea on paper" to "application on web." Many of us have enjoyed the great satisfaction of seeing our plans come to fruition.

But for many of us our B2B projects, especially our first one, run into problems. We haven't yet learned where the unexpected bumps will be. We haven't been careful with some things. We didn't know we had to be careful! We are giving it our best shot, but we just "don't know what we don't know." Those "emotional investments" come with a personal price.

It is not as hard as it seems to anticipate problems. The best way to start anticipating problems is to get the conversation going with your team and identifying their concerns. This can be done in a brainstorming session. An independent, third party can facilitate it if you wish. This is particularly important if you may be part of the problem. Even if you don't perceive yourself to be part of the problem, however, it is never a bad idea to have the brainstorming session facilitated. It gives you a chance to participate more fully and to take detailed notes of the conversations and exchange of views. You can also probe for understanding in a different way, such as asking questions in such a way that it helps the facilitator who is "scribing" problems on a flip chart gain a better understanding. You can concentrate on ideas instead of penmanship.

If your management style hasn't been participatory or particularly open in the past, this is a way to break through to a more creative work environment.

Perform risk assessments for each project. Having completed some brainstorming to anticipate problems, your next task will be to do a risk assessment for your project. You may have thought that the brainstorming was your risk assessment, but it was not. What you will have is a collection of "hopes and fears." You will have a jumble of potential problems.

Some will be issues with which you have to deal, like how the team is communicating, which may have little bearing on risk. Some things from your brainstorming you will find could never occur. Other things will be so minor that they pose no real risk. They aren't to be taken lightly and just laughed off; they may be sincere concerns by members of the team that, in fact, pose no immediate threat to this particular project. The last items that should not be included are items that are outside of your company's control or sphere of influence (such as the stock markets collapse, wars, catastrophic weather).

Other things from your brainstorming will have a direct bearing. These are the ones on which to concentrate with a risk assessment.

There are a few, fundamental questions and answers that you need to identify:

❑ In a few words, what is the issue or problem?

❑ How likely is this problem to occur? (On a scale from 1-low to 10-high).

❑ If you don't mitigate the risk and the problem does occur, how severe would it be? (On a scale from 1-low to 10-high).

❑ Identify (crisply) three things that need to be done to mitigate the risk. These have to be realistic actions, which are sufficiently "resourced" (people, money, tools, time) to be complete in the timeframe needed.

❑ Identify who will be responsible for mitigating the risk (one and only one person for each of the three things needed to mitigate).

❑ Identify dates when the risk will by mitigated and dates for key milestones (one or more for each of the three things needed to mitigate).

❑ If you do all the mitigation actions, by the dates identified, what is the likelihood the problem will still occur? (On a scale from 1-low to 10-high. 8-10 should be showstoppers to the project going forward).

❑ If you do all the mitigation actions, by the dates identified, what is the likelihood the problem will be catastrophic or significant? (On a scale from 1-low to 10-high. 5 and above should give management "acid indigestion.")

Mitigate means "to make milder;" it doesn't mean to make go away. We typically don't have sufficient resources to make the entire potential problem or all our problems disappear. But we can anticipate and plan to make them milder and survivable.

Like with my woodman's dome, through this process you can place what's important in the hands of people who care. You can take the advice of those around you who have more or different experience, like the advice my mother had given me. You vividly demonstrate the concern you have and the importance this issue has for your company.

You can identify the risk, put the answers to the above questions into a spreadsheet, and monitor them as your project progresses. You may choose to post these on a bulletin board or discuss them frequently at your team meetings. Make these visible and constant on your mind.

Write "broken scenarios" into your use case or business plan. If you write use cases for your projects, you can document secondary, exception, and alternative scenarios to cover the handling of planned alternate routes. In these you identify planned exceptional events or choices that a user may follow. That works fine for application process design and some user aids ("cheat sheets" and "job aids").

But for other unplanned events you will want to identify "broken scenarios." In these you can document unplanned activities and events that can and do periodically occur for which you will not have a specific alternative path and design (but where you can provide a bit of direction). They are "broken" from the standpoint that they cannot be documented to the last detail and usually not even to a conclusion point (nor should they). But they can provide valuable insights into the business process.

For example, let's say you are running a grocery store. You might have a use case that describes how you scan items at the cash register and another on how you key in the prices at the cash register. You might have secondary, exception, and alterative scenarios to handle things like missing price information, items broken at the cash register, credit card processing, etc. The list of alternative paths can go on and on and you can document the typical use case to follow the process for handling each one. At some point, all of the above will happen and may happen every day in the course of running your grocery store.

You should also write a "broken scenario" for if the electricity is interrupted. When that occurs, your concern shifts from the checkout process to one of security, safety, and restoration. Your case may be conditional, based on the time of day it occurs. Near closing may be different from the middle of the day.

Writing "broken scenarios" can provide valuable insights and raise interesting questions that you may be able to incorporate in your design: "Should I have flashlights at the register?" or "Do I need uninterrupted power supply?" This thought process is highly transferable to our B2B applications.

If you don't write use cases, consider documenting this in your business planning activities. These can be valuable materials to help in production support and in system recovery.

Anticipating problems allows us to circumvent them where possible. If I had thought my globe could have been broken, maybe I would of taken my mother's advice more seriously.

But even when we cannot get around our problems entirely, anticipating the implications and starting the recovery as soon as possible can be helpful.

"The problem is not that there are problems. The problem is expecting otherwise and thinking that having problems is a problem."

Theodore Rubin

Clean Up Your Own Mess

He was a short, medium build Mexican. He had jet-black hair, graying slightly at the sides. His neatly ironed kaki colored shirts and work pants had pronounced creases. He always had a smile on his face and always seemed happy. It was as if he was above and beyond the circumstances of his daily toil.

His name was on a label on his shirt: Manuel. We called him Mr. Manny and he was always working-- never at a furious pace, but steady. Concentrating so much on the task at hand he could ignore all the kids swirling around him if he needed to, but never so much that he didn't have a warm smile for us at an opportune moment.

He would do anything: sweeping, plumbing, changing light bulbs, and waxing floors. He obviously enjoyed kids. Only later did it occur to me that he might have had children or grandchildren at the school. I never knew. But work was work and he admired all of us from afar. Maybe he appreciated education more than most people. Maybe he understood a role can be important, even if it is a small role.

Usually there was glitter or pieces of construction paper on the floor by the end of the school day in my kindergarten classroom. Extraneous white glue was always left on the chairs and tables when we left class. But by the next morning Mr. Manny would have set everything right again.

I remember once knocking over a tray of watercolors. We had been painting at the tables and I was concentrating on my masterpiece. We were cleaning out our brushes in the community water jar. I guess I was concentrating so much on my artwork that I hadn't noticed the jar had mysteriously moved toward the edge of the table, when I elbowed it to the floor. Luckily, I didn't break the jar. Miss Waters sprinted from where Clean Up Your Own Mess she had been helping someone, to the towel dispenser, and then to the spill. When she realized the water had spread quite a long way across the floor, she told me to get a mop from Mr. Manny.

I went down to the janitors' room where Mr. Manny was working on something. I told him what had happened and he just gave me a slight, knowing smile. He must have seen this scene a million times. He pulled over a bucket on wheels that was already filled with soapy water and a mop (hum, well prepared. This must occur frequently.). Without saying much, I walked behind him as he pushed the mop to the back of the room where all my classmates had been prior to my accident. They had gone on to other work and left the scene of the crime.

I began to join my classmates. After all, Mr. Manny had his job and I had mine. Surely he could finish that little job in no time. He caught me by the collar and asked, "Where are you going? You have to clean up your own mess." He handed me the mop and stood by while I mopped the floor to his satisfaction (well, somewhat). He pointed out spots that needed greater attention. When I finished, I returned to the front of the room and he rolled the bucket away. That may have been the most important lesson I learned that day: "You have to clean up your own mess."

eBusiness is no different. You have to clean up your own mess. In the high pressure created by the "get it done" attitude of today's business climate we often rush off to the next project and the next activity. When we have done something wrong, for example, designing a process incorrectly, we sometimes just move on to the next project. We need to bear in mind that we can leave a large wake behind us.

Frequently, it takes months for us to discover that what we have put in place isn't quite right. Maybe we haven't clearly understood what the customer wanted. Maybe the "mock-up" didn't quite live up to customer expectations. Maybe we didn't test for a certain way the customer was going to use the tool. That often happens where we haven't fully appreciated the workflow the customer will be using. It also happens when the customer process changes as a result of the new tool: "I was going to use the packing memo for input. But then I realized that I could just as easily enter the data at the receiving dock itself. In order to do that the layout needs to be changed a bit."

Use post-implementation validation. When giving a speech, we are often told: "Tell them what you are going to tell them. Tell them. Tell them what you told them." With a twist, that is pretty good advice in determining whether your work has stayed on course. "Tell them what you are going to do. Do it. Ask them if you did what you said you were going to do."

It is essential they you tell them clearly and specifically what you intend to do and when. You need to tell them in very general terms what you intend to do over the next six months or so. Advise them of what limitations you already have seen and the concerns that you have with the schedule as well. Then tell them specifically what you are going to be doing in the next project. This needs to be as specific as possible.

Leave them with documentation, conceptual drawings, project timelines, and use case materials where appropriate. Tell them the roadblocks that are ahead of you. If appropriate, ask for specific help, such as in piloting or in further review work. Listen specifically for their concerns and don't be surprised if their concerns are not your concerns and if they don't have issues with the problems that are keeping you awake at night.

As you do your project, keep them abreast of your progress and how your timeline may be shifting. Explain the reasoning behind any shifts in date or functionality. It is important that they be crystal clear as to when they need to participate and what is expected of both of you. This is still building the foundation and helping define what it is that you will be delivering. In essence, this will define even "if" you have a mess. It is the blueprint against which you will come to conclusion in cleaning up your mess.

If you do not have this blueprint ready, additional functionality can slip into your design. These can be features you don't wish to create or are not ready to create. "Oh, I thought it was going to work such and such way."

There are two types of errors that can creep into your project: 1) errors of design and development, and 2) errors of understanding.

Finally, as you stabilize your application, plan on evaluating your success from your trading partners' viewpoint. Ask them if it met their needs and if it does what it was intended to do. If you have done a good job telling them what you are going to do and executing against the plan, there should be few surprises. Sometimes you will need to do some mopping up. The application may not perform the way everyone thought it would. It may take longer to complete certain tasks or appear on the web page in an unexpected fashion. This can certainly happen with the wide variety of browsers that are in use and the various ways they handle language standards.

This post-implementation validation can also help identify follow-on features that will enhance the users experience and better support the business process. But it is mandatory that you view those suggested changes in the context of the original use case. Otherwise, once again you run the risk of adding additional complexity or building features that are outside the intent of the original design.

Don't just send out surveys to attempt to collect this information. You want to collect this feedback in person where possible. This allows you to see the body language and drive deeper than is otherwise possible. The added bonus is that if you do this in person and you have had a spectacular success you get to receive the congratulations in a more personal way. This helps cement your trading partner relationship, builds trust, and propels you forward toward the next successful project.

Think about production support requirements early. It is easier to clean your mess if you have the mop and bucket ready. In the struggle to get job aids, training materials, and the like in place for your start-up, it is important to sort out who will be responsible for production support and what types of support they will provide. It is not always clear how the "hand offs" will take place and how production problems will be tracked and managed.

If you don't want to embarrass yourself in front of your customers, work through these during your application-testing phase. Perform "dry runs" of production support. Start by asking yourself the question, "Who will know about the problem first and who should they contact?" This will lead to additional questions, such as what additional training is required, what tools should be used, and how problems will escalate.

Map out how the problems will be handled and passed as they go from "generic" problems (such as who the trading partner contacts for questions) to technically specific (i.e., "level 3" type of support).

Finally, confirm with your trading partners before start-up if this type of support will meet their needs. Publish appropriate documents (web pages, flow diagrams, etc.) and refresh these documents using scheduled, periodic reviews.

Plan on rework. Think of rework as the natural sequence of things. Clean up is merely continuous work improvement. The Sistine Chapel needs a touch up every once in a while. Michelangelo doesn't seem to mind.

As part of the budgeting process, we need to plan for rework.

If you have a plan in place for cleaning up your own mess, the problems you encounter will not seem as dire. You will know the steps to go through and will have confidence that you will be able to bring the resources to bear to resolve them quickly and efficiently. Not being prepared can become a stumbling block to your overall effort. The sense of urgency (or outright panic) will draw away resources for the more important, long range projects that you are working on. It will defocus your effort and increase the probability that those future projects will also struggle.

When you make a mess (and you will) be prepared to clean it up.

The urgent problems are seldom the important ones.

Dwight D. Eisenhower

Setting Limits

I remember leaning against the chain link fence just watching the older children play. The fence was short-- probably only four feet tall. It wouldn't have prevented an adult from climbing over. That wasn't its purpose. There was a larger chain link fence for that purpose, which stretched the border of the schoolyard and ran along the path of the sidewalks around the school.

This fence had one purpose. It prevented the kindergarteners from mixing with the other children at Mulberry Elementary School. It was a safety zone within a safety zone. We couldn't escape or wander into the playground of the larger kids. We were confined to a small area where our teachers could keep tabs on us. We were not at risk of enduring the large kids' roughhousing or their pranks. We were not at risk of inadvertently being knocked down or lost in the shuffle of many running children. We were safe and secure.

The older children at school were protected by the small fence as well. They didn't have to worry about stepping on us. They didn't worry about getting in trouble for their carelessness. They were free to frolic on the playground and expend their excess energy.

The short fence set a limit for all of us. The limit was appropriate and necessary.

Businesses often view the world with today's glasses. They think in terms of today's issues and struggle to inch their thinking forward. They ask their customers what they want to do and end up automating today's problem. They end up attempting to automate the cow paths.

New communications mechanisms lend themselves to rethinking. I love the story attributed to Alexander Graham Bell that he initially envisioned one telephone in every city. After all, wasn't the communication mechanism the telephone would largely displace the telegraph? And didn't people go to the telegraph office to communicate. So, why wouldn't our thinking about the telephone initially go down the same path? Far too often in B2B our thinking is based in the present.

Think of how different the world would have been if Bell had executed his grand vision of one telephone per city. We might have millions of phones instead of a billion. If his implementation had gotten only that far along, it may have prevented the ubiquitous device we enjoy today. We run a real danger when our B2B solutions don't go far enough.

And when our thinking isn't in the present, it is typically too far off into the future. We try to go from unautomated to over automated! We move from "little or nothing" to unrealistically big--there generally is no middle ground.

I love to watch business units attempt to put together their eBusiness plans. It follows a similar path each time. Inveritably, they lay out a scope of functionality that could choke a horse. They come to the party with a rosy picture in mind of everything they want to do. Money's no object. They've read all the magazines, watched the television commercials, and seen all the sales brochures. It all looks so simple-- on paper and on the tube.

I recently ran into it again in our procurement area: "We'll just tell the suppliers what they have to do," was coming out of their mouths. Interesting. In an area where we should have so much leverage and control, we still haven't gotten beyond twenty-five percent penetration in twenty-years of trying with our suppliers. Why? Because it is like raising children. Each time you are thinking, "We'll just tell them what they have to do," you are about to get a new lesson in parenting! We attempt to leap to a solution that is far beyond what we could accomplish. B2B lends itself to two types of change: incremental change, where we make many small steps toward a final vision, and substantial, reengineered change, where we make quantum leaps toward that vision.

But mostly businesses try to do three other types of change:

1. Window dressing changes. Move to the web "to modernize." "Get with it" mentality. Pave the cow path. No substantive change to the business process. No questioning value, function or necessity. "Were just moving it to the web to give greater access."

2. Massive change, without reengineering. "Boil the ocean" mentality. Out with the old and in with the new. Change everything! Everything we have done before is bad. While the behaviors say "but don't really change anything, because we really like it the way it is, so don't ruffle any feathers. Don't do anything to make anyone uncomfortable."

3. Politics is king. No single person is given the reins. Everyone has veto power. Nobody really has a say, because everybody has a say. In the end, when all is said and done, not much is done.

The earmarks of the two that can be successful: vision. The earmarks of the three than cannot be successful: lack of vision at the outset.

The best eBusiness projects I have seen have incorporated Business Process Reengineering (BPR). But my experience has been that BPR works best when desperation has set in. When your back is to the wall, you take it seriously. I think the same may be true with both business strategies and eBusiness strategies; you get it right when you have to get it right. Other times you just play. Oh, you might luck out every once in a while, but not consistently.

I have been involved in two reengineered B2B processes. Both have been wildly successful. I have been involved in dozens of B2B projects that didn't reengineer the business process. The results have been a "mixed bag." Does that mean to insure success of your B2B implementation you have to reengineer? No. It may not be appropriate, but it is worthy of serious consideration.

Much as we try, you can't "boil the ocean." It is only natural for us to seek to go beyond what can realistically be achieved. Humans are by nature "dreamers." We can see a better world before us. It is so real in our dreams we can taste it. "If only we can align part a with section b," we think to ourselves.

Sometimes we try to do too much. We try to "boil the ocean." No amount of human effort could ever pull that off.

There is goodness in dreaming and planning for a better B2B future. It is really how all progress is made and how all new things come into being. Without a dream of high levels of defense security, the Internet never would have been born. Without a dream of universal connectivity, the web wouldn't have been created.

The dream of "cyberspace" came long before its reality. William Gibson coined the term "cyberspace" in his 1984 science fiction novel <u>Neuromancer</u>. John Perry Barlow became the first person to apply the term to the online world, while participating in an online discussion on The Well in 1990.

But the dream didn't merely spring into reality. Step-by-step, sometimes planned and sometimes by accident, the pieces came together. Each small step, building upon the base of the previous steps, was to become a new foundation for the next small step. This is how you need to think and plan for your B2B projects. This is how real progress comes about.

We have to set limits to each new step. They should be small, definable, achievable steps along the long path to success. Confined to what can be achieved, we establish an interim goal.

Many of the factors that will determine your chance for success are in your control, but not all of them. Factors initially outside your control may include trading partner concerns and resistance, technology, and security conditions. You work through each problem one at a time.

We don't need to be able to see each step. But we do have to have a reasonable probability that they can be conquered. Here are two examples. My project may be "road blocked" by trading partner resistance. After hearing the concerns, I may conclude that we can work through the issues without making systemic changes to the proposed solution. My next step is to alleviate the concern. I set a limit on simultaneous or subsequent steps, because they may give my trading partners a contradictory signal. They may be telling the trading partner that I am not concerned with his feelings and concerns and will "bull forward" with my solution. So I intentionally hold off doing some steps, until I am confident I have laid the right foundation.

The second example is a project that we had where we had concerns with security in some Microsoft products. I didn't have any control over how Microsoft would deal with the issues, whether they would deal with them at all, or in what timeframe they would deal with the problem. I had to limit my choices to 1) wait or 2) look for another solution. But it certainly was prudent for me to establish some limits so that I didn't box myself into a corner.

Don't develop features beyond "your interest." Kodak is risk adverse. It seemed we would never be leading edge at anything (other than possibly some areas of product development). We had to see that the business tools were ready. We have to assess, assess, assess before we would act. It was just their nature and probably still is.

Sometimes I thought we will never get to where we need to go. Frustrating as that may have been for me personally, it was our reality. I had to live within those confines. Those were the limits of the company, based on their operational model and heritage.

I can, and do, continually push against this risk adversity. Sometimes I succeed in "pushing out the fence." But I also know it is a confine with which I will probably always have to contend. I also recognize there is some goodness in this seeming limitation. It establishes the ground rules under which I develop B2B activities. It is the fence that limits my arena of work and protects me from wandering too far "a field" from what will be accepted.

In 2003 I working on a pilot for Collaborative Planning, Forecasting and Replenishment* (CPFR). This was not a new methodology, nor were the software offerings for doing CPFR particularly new or risky. People had been doing CPFR for quite a while already, more of it as pilots than robust business applications. We had heard modest interest in CPFR "come and go" from our customers, but nobody had really demanded that we implement.

What we failed to consider, as a company, is that CPFR may have benefited us more than our customers. There could be a strategic advantage to link the supply chain from customer through to supplier. This may have been an opportunity staring us in the face.

Realistically, CPFR was not our number one priority. We were not ready for such a dramatic change in our supply chain operating model. CPFR had to season and mature to a certain point. We had to achieve a certain level of confidence before our management was ready to move forward.

I could have spent years making myself hoarse, continually singing the praises of CPFR. Or I could have worked on higher priority initiatives, while periodically raising the interest in CPFR and reassessing our business readiness.

Setting the limit allowed us to give our first priority efforts the attention they needed, while allowing the secondary priorities time to mature. Once they become the top priority interests, they can be given our full attention.

We need to reestablish our priorities and identify our trade-offs frequently. We only have to be able to see down to the next bend in the road. We really don't have to lay out the five-year plan in intricate detail. It doesn't do much good to try. There are only two types of estimates of the unforeseen B2B future: wrong and lucky.

That next bend in the road may be the next budget cycle or planning horizon. It is better to do something of less scope extremely well than to do something very broad, which is also poorly done.

You don't have to have all the answers before you start. You rarely have answers to many of the questions. You generally only need to know which direction you are going.

If eBusiness is going to be a way of life for you and your company, then why rush to get everything up and running? Do a few things well. Let a couple of projects "sell" your program to your customers and yourself.

There is nothing wrong with working with your customers to determine the path of implementation. You probably want to narrow it down to only the next two quarters, however. Both of you may see a need to go off in a totally different directions. And you probably don't want to be very specific.

But you need to do enough work so that you understand what each other values. Enough so you can evaluate business benefits for your trading partners and yourselves. You want to bundle developments together and time sequence them in an agreeable fashion. Invoices with payments. Orders and advance shipment notice.

If you say you want to do electronic order entry, for example, that's easy. Maybe too easy. It is when you say you want to have a browser based order entry process that operates in real time to the back office application, accurately giving price and delivery date in less than one second per line item. Now that's hard. But it is probably the level of functionality you want to develop. Not too small and not too large, but stretching your abilities.

Laying out your plans too far in advance is like going to a restaurant and ordering your salad, soup, entrée, vegetables, after dinner coffee, dessert for your next six meals all at the same time. It doesn't work very well. After I have eaten my main course, based on my mood and disposition, I want to decide on coffee and dessert...and for this meal only.

It doesn't matter that you have twenty projects on your "to do list"; you can only do one or two at a time well. You risk a "conflicting" design--one function handled one way and another in a contrary way. So limit yourself to a few things.

The limits you set need to include a lower limit and an upper limit. When you approach the upper limit, you need to step back and determine if a fundamental change is needed. If so, suspend your activities and reengineer the business process.

It is when we fence in our projects that we bound out failure. We bound out additional complexity and risk. We keep our attention focused on what will make us successful.

"You can never plan the future by the past."

Edmund Burke

* Collaborative Planning, Forecasting and Replenishment® and CPFR® are Registered Trade Marks of the Voluntary Interindustry Commerce Standards (VICS) association.

We All Need Encouragement

At first, I thought she just wanted to please Miss Waters. Then I thought she wanted attention. Then I realized that was the way Robin was--very helpful. Always!

When you sat at her table she wanted to make sure that everyone had the colored pencil they liked and that the pencils were sharp enough for everyone. If not, she would pull a plastic pencil sharpener and napkin out of her pocket and sharpen the pencil while neatly piling the shavings on the napkin. When she was done, she would quietly and neatly roll up the napkin and throw it away.

She would make sure we all had enough paper. She wouldn't just take her sheets and pass the stack along like the rest of us would. She would distribute one to each personal individually. She wasn't flashy about it. She just quietly distributed the papers or pencils or crayons or whatever. Miss Waters never said a word to her when she would get out of her seat to help others. If that had been me, I would have been ordered back to my seat! I guess Miss Waters recognized that that was just the way Robin was.

Of course, this always made her last in finishing projects, but she never seemed to mind. But what I really remember about Robin is that when we would finish our projects, she would stop and take a good look at what we had done and tell us what she liked about our pictures, and then drift back to her own work. She never failed to take notice. She never failed to tell us what she liked.

I can imagine her today, organizing church picnics, arranging multiple family vacations, and helping out with the Girl Scouts and soccer teams. Working behind the scenes to make sure everything was "just right." But I bet she also encourages her kids and all the kids she encounters to do their best.

Teaching skills by demonstration. Teaching character by example.

eBusiness can be an uncomfortable space. I remember attending a class on EDI in the early 1990s. Two hours into the class, at the first morning break, the instructor pointed out that we were now all in the 99th percentile of business people in understanding electronic commerce. Interesting revelation, but I doubted it could possibly be true. It took me a few months to realize that it was true. There is so much misunderstanding of what eBusiness is all about that it is almost embarrassing.

Most people think it is about saving money and there certainly is an aspect of cost savings. But that is like saying golf is about making the lowest score. Certainly, if you are good enough, you can make a low score. For most of us, making a low score without being outdoors, enjoying the beauty of a spring day, getting exercise, and cavorting with our friends would be a very shallow experience indeed.

eBusiness is about relationships. I have never seen a greater opportunity to get close to your customers and suppliers than with eBusiness. But I have also never seen so many opportunities get close but slip between our fingers. The reality is that we can save far more money if we work together to do eBusiness than in devising our strategies in a vacuum and trying to convince our trading partners that it is a good thing for them (no matter how good for them it may actually be).

We can also streamline processes and gain a feel of "slaying the dragons" in our business. We have opportunities to rethink our business models and toss out those things that no longer make a great deal of sense. But eBusiness is not a panacea. It is very hard work. Never mind the advertisements that make it look so simple: "Buy our eBusiness application server...life will be good."

Potential trading partners are crying out for help. They are looking for solutions. They are looking for new opportunities. But they typically don't know where to start. The starting point is not pulling together a bunch of vendors to do "request for proposals." The starting point is sharpening your pencils and getting down to the hard work of figuring out your opportunities. But we need the help and encouragement of others along the way.

We all need to mentor <u>and</u> be mentored. We all need to mentor. My father used to point out that the best way to reinforce something you have learned was to teach someone else. We have a responsibility to pass along what we learn and experience. We need to share our insights. We need to be willing enough to share our successes and brave enough to share our failures. We need to help each other up and over the learning curve. Without this sharing going on in our companies our trading partners recognize a lack of depth. They see inconsistencies in our approach and our confidence. Every day we have an opportunity to share and reinforce our experiences with our co-workers. Every day we have the opportunity to sharpen each other and reinforce what we have learned and, more importantly, share <u>why</u> it is important.

We can use either formal or informal methods to mentor those junior to us. It doesn't have to be a well documented and largely regulated activity, though that can bring discipline to mentoring. But it needs to be regular and consistent.

We all have things we can learn from others. These can be outside of the traditional boundaries of eBusiness, such as with team building or learning the financial evaluations common to a solid business case. There are always others around who can share their expertise, if we are willing to tap into other people.

We need champions. I have never seen an eBusiness strategy "bubble-up" from the bottom. I have read about it occurring once or twice, but have never seen it take place myself. By sheer force of will, chance, or luck some managers have gotten the attention of the senior management to make something happen. Well, not in my experience.

It is akin to pulling oneself up by the bootstrap. It is probably not physically impossible, but not very likely to occur.

More commonly, I have seen businesses "assign" the task of defining the eBusiness strategy to an individual or small team. Universally, these don't have the breadth of vision that is required. They also don't have the level of commitment required to prepare and execute the plans against the strategy. Most of these are dead on arrival; we just don't recognize they are dead.

A champion can carry the banner for your initiative. A champion can gain access to the decision makers at your company. He or she can get the right people in the organization to drive your eBusiness strategies to complement your general business strategies. They can point out the business case and keep attention focused on the decisions at hand.

The best champion I ever saw was a whisperer!

He wasn't flashy about making formal presentations. He didn't show off nor was he "fluffed up" about working with senior levels of management every day. Instead, he would sit next to the key decision makers and during presentations he would lean over and whisper a few words that would "connect" the presentation to the decision makers' real world problems and concerns.

He might, for example, be watching a presentation that talked about reducing cost for supporting small businesses and lean over and say, "Have you thought about how Joe might apply this?" Joe might have been the last guy on the other person's mind. He might have been focused on some other activity a million miles away.

He would guide the process to the right conclusion. He would "bump" the process along by nurturing as well as confining, to maintain focus. Just like herding cattle; keep them moving down the path and not wandering astray.

A key role for the champion is to keep management's attention focused on the task at hand. There are so many issues to work through and so many demands placed on the key decision makers at our companies that somebody needs to help frame and focus the eBusiness initiatives. That is the job of the champion. He confines both subject matter and timeframe. The encourages the management process along.

He may or may not be the sponsor to your B2B initiatives, but he will play a vital role in your success.

We all need to be a cheerleader. The everyday tasks of eBusiness can drain us of energy. The demands of short-term projects can weigh on us. We need a cheerleader to keep us encouraged. This person can point out the importance of our activities, just when we are gutting out the most mundane details. They show us the peaks when we are in the valleys. They demonstrate for us that success in climbing the mountain is not in running up the hill, but in small, continuous steps.

We all need Robins in our lives. People to encourage us, exhort us, and cheer us. People to mentor us and help us along. People to play the champion and the cheerleader.

They sustain and strengthen us. They are really the giants among us.

"You get the best out of others when you give the best of yourself."

Harry Firestone

Teamwork and Cooperation

Most of them lived on my street and many within five doors of my house. They were the kids I always played with when I was in kindergarten: Gary Oien, Harold Comstock, Brian Williams, and Duane Takota.

We had our own established unwritten neighborhood rules, relationships, and considerations. Not everyone liked to do everything I liked. Harold could care less about baseball, so when we felt like playing "over the line" he had other things to do. You didn't ask Harold to play baseball more than once. Nor did you "rag" at him because he didn't like baseball.

Gary liked to draw and watch television when we were inside, but didn't care for "make believe" or board games. Brian had a clubhouse in his backyard and when we tired of playing outdoors, that was a ready place to play. We knew each other's interests. We knew each other's skills and abilities, like what position everyone preferred when choosing sides for baseball.

We didn't pressure anyone to play and we naturally formed teams when the time came to play certain games. These were guys you could trust to play with you the way you wanted to play.

When we started kindergarten, we didn't play my favorite games while at school. We played other games that were either conducive to small places (such as the playground in the kindergarten area) or large spaces (like the big kids playground, where we would play kickball and where ball getting by the outfielder meant it would go for "miles"). We played games that involved the girls more frequently at school.

I made new friends who had different interests and played games I had never seen before. For some of the games that we did play, they introduced a never-ending variety of new rules. I wasn't sure how some of these rules were fair, but we learned to compromise, adapt and create new teams.

I am still compromising, adapting and creating new teams. The rules are still changing around me.

B2B creates new models of customer and supply interaction. As we straighten out the supply and information chains at our companies, relationships have to adjust. No longer do we live in a world where I am insulated and just do "my portion" of the process. New collaborative models have shaken the foundations of business and have challenged what "my portion" really is. With frequency customers show up on our doorsteps to see why we are doing some things in certain ways. Their creativity is boundless and they challenge our thinking. Sometimes they just want to pass cost or responsibility to someone else. Other times, they want to look at the overall process flow to see if there is a better way of doing work.

In either event, going back in a collaborate fashion to look at the business model is healthy and helpful. This requires teamwork and honesty. That honesty extends inwardly into our companies as well as out to our trading partners. Sometimes you will recognize that "nobody" is able to solve the problem that befuddles you. Other times you will find that what you thought was the problem isn't the root cause. Sometimes you will walk away without making a change or coming to agreement on what should be changed. But there are those "golden moments" when you can make a fundamental breakthrough.

The accomplishment feels different when you have done it honestly, openly, and in a collaborative fashion. Your pride in what you have done extends beyond your own walls. Now your partner is happy with the situation and this can lead to future efforts and new directions.

Playing with new partners. Learning to "play" with new partners parallels the first weeks of kindergarten. With B2B we continually have new vendors and new "customers." Sometimes the external customers are the same, but we deal with new names and faces at those customer locations who have responsibility in the B2B domain. This can strengthen the overall relationship in a very complementary manner. For example, where we have traditionally worked with order management and over the years have built relationships and trust, we can sometimes use those relationships to break through problems in B2B. Sometimes it works in a reverse fashion as well.

Many times when we are having trouble getting to a key contact in a retailer's purchasing or supply chain operations, for example, we can go through their EDI team. Those groups command attention in most retailers, as they play a pivotal role in the smooth running of their operations.

The point is this: crossing through boundaries has a multiplication effect. The relationship can be more than doubled in strength.

B2B can also bring forward brand new trading partners and relationships. In businesses that previously resisted EDI as too costly or complex, for example, they may be more willing to look into XML. They don't see (and don't need to see) that there is not a great deal of difference in cost or complexity between the two, contrary to the trade literature. The issue, however, is making a relationship breakthrough, not a technology choice.

Teamwork and cooperation is king. It requires a steady management hand to steer the B2B ship. With the frantic pace of development required and the need to keep a clear eye out for competitive changes, resources need to continually be shifting. This requires cooperation among the team members so that they don't too narrowly focus their skills in one area. But it also requires a commitment to train and nurture people in areas that may be foreign and threatening to them.

All members of the team need to be valued for their individual contributions. But the team needs to recognize (and be recognized for) their ability to fill the voids that will inveritably be recognized later in the project. The phase "not my job" should be outlawed on B2B projects. It needs to be "our job" to fill the gaps.

How do we get there? What gets measured gets done-- that includes soft skills, such as teamwork and cooperation. Establish and continually assess the ability of the team to work together. Encourage members to play together outside work in social activities as well business settings. The establishment of trust among team members is essential. Don't be overly critical during the early stages of team building when we often have to "storm" to create a team. Allow a healthy amount of conflict, as long as the intention is to bring the team together. When the conflict becomes "personal" or divisive, nip the problem in the bud.

Sometimes you will need to take unorthodox steps to bring team members together. I had two members of a team who were continually complaining about each other. What I recognized is that they had complementary skills and that they were really not sufficiently aware of what the other did. This was a team of around twenty-five people and, over the years, the two people had moved further apart physically, to the point that they eventually were on opposite ends of the office.

What was the fix to the problem? I made them cube mates! People thought I was crazy. I heard more that one remark about "being an accomplice to murder."

When they started to show up on my doorstep to complain about one another, I turned them around and told them to try to make it work and that I was counting on them as a team to work it out. Soon (actually, remarkably soon) I had one come to me to comment how valuable the other person was and what a great job they did. I about fell out of my chair! I retained sufficient composure to complement them on their team effort. Soon they were lunching together and they were able to handle their pet peeves in a lighthearted way.

B2B brings about change-- sometimes at a furious rate. Teams need to form and dissolve quickly. Cooperation needs to be a badge of honor. We need to respect and honor those who can collect us together and give us cohesion toward a single goal. Don't confuse this with management-- teamwork takes leadership.

"The important thing to recognize is that it takes a team, and the team ought to get credit for the wins and the losses. Successes have many fathers, failures have none."

Philip Caldwell

Graduation to First Grade

Moms cry on the first and the last day of kindergarten. It always has been and always will be. It is part of their job description.

They grieve the baby and toddler who has suddenly become a child before their eyes as they enter kindergarten. Then they grieve the kindergartener who has graduated to "the grades." They spring forward in their minds to high school and college graduations to come. Then weddings. Then the day this child will bring his or her own child to kindergarten. "How quickly they grow up."

It is a circle that rolls from generation to generation back to the distant past. It is something all of us have lived and observed.

Tears celebrate every major life change: births, graduations, weddings, having our own children, and deaths. They signal the "veering off points" of our lives...when one life situation ends and another begins, such as when we went from not having children to having children. Tears of joy. Tears of fear. Tears are a symbol of change.

At the end of kindergarten we had a large party in our classroom. There were cookies, cupcakes, and punch. Mothers swarmed over us with pride and loving care. They laughed and smiled and hugged each other. You would have thought they were graduating! My mom cried. Tears came easily to my mother and I thank God she passed that on to me.

There were only two times a year when the gate between the big kids' playground and the kindergarteners' playground was left open: Halloween and graduation day. For the kindergarteners, graduation day was great fun.

There are two things we most looked forward to on that day: visiting the classrooms we would be in the following year and, our final ceremony, the last recess-- when we played on the big kids' playground for the first time.

When the school day was drawing to a close we stood at the gate, fidgeting and waiting for our principal, Mr. Wright, to release us for recess on the big kids' playground. He stood looking at us, smiled, and swung the gate open. But we stood there in silence for a long time. Until he simply said, "What are you waiting for?"

We have neither tears nor diplomas to mark our readiness to take eBusiness seriously. We don't recognize the "veering off point" that should be occurring. So we need to muster the strength and determination to start out on our own. We have to tell ourselves that now is the time.

Too often I observe companies just "tinkering" when it comes to B2B. While we talk, we consult, we prototype, and we pilot, we are merely standing and watching the gate that has swung open.

We do "activities" that get in the way of real progress. We "think" we know where we are going, but we don't demonstrate either the belief or confidence that we do.

It is as if we collectively fear to step out in a bold way.

Change is something all of us experience and all of us resist. In the eBusiness world over the last years we have see titanic changes taking place around us. Some of the changes have been exciting and others have been frightening.

With B2B we have seen startling changes-- on a level never experienced before in business. Ever.

People who saw the dot.com meltdown as the end of eBusiness were looking at one very, very, very small battle in a much larger war. They bring a warped sense of reality and totally miss the opportunity that is still before us. The risks and battles have only begun. There will be more meltdowns on the road to success. But there will be success.

We have observed new tools and methods of communication that have changed our lives-- sometimes for the better and sometimes not. I am nearly overwhelmed with the number of emails I receive every day. Twenty years ago, when it was more novelty than tool, it was quite interesting to get an email. In recent years it has become a ubiquitous business tool. How did we ever do without it?

When we first started using emails they were more like a replacement for letters. One-to-one or one-to-few communications. Then tools came along that made some emails more like newspapers. That stage was nearly perfect in my eyes-- lots of "personalized" emails with a sprinkling of selected news.

More recently tools have come along to blast emails at us. One-to-many. Misdirected. Largely pointless. Inconvenient. The originators of these emails are killing off the milk cow and don't know it. The have anesthetized us to their own message. Many emails are easier to trash than read.

With those tools have come other tools--filters to fend off the noise. A good change, followed by a bad change, followed by another change that seems like it shouldn't even be necessary. Change again and again in a never-ending stream of change.

Change before us can freeze us from action. Change barrages us with messages: "Not yet!" "Wait for the next change!" "First, see where things are headed!" When, in fact, we need to be wading in.

In our day-to-day eBusiness lives we live where the tides of change ebb and flow. We don't work in the safe harbors. We work were the waves crash to shore, where its power is always awesome and sometimes overwhelming.

Some forces move us to change and others forces cause us to resist. We are faced with a choice. Like a pier that takes the beating of the waves for long stretches of time we can ultimately succumb.

If we are not careful, it is easy for us to stand on the shoreline and watch, thinking, "It will not hit me." Or we can have the courage to wade in.

A law of physics can be applied to B2B. Newton's First Law of physics states: "If a body is at rest, it will continue at rest unless acted upon by a net external force."

So it is with B2B.

We stand at rest behind the gate. We stand where we think it is safe. We busy ourselves with prototypes and pilots. We hire consultants, we study, we evaluate. We wait for the optimal software or perfect business conditions before we will act. There is a time and place for each of those activities, but "enough is enough."

We need to time box those distractions and put ourselves in motion. If we don't, someone else will. When they do we may not be successful in reacting to these external threats.

We need to ask ourselves, "What are we waiting for?" Has the time come for you to take eBusiness seriously?

Is it time to venture onto the big kids' playground?

Sure-- we are going to get scraped. Expect a few bandages.

Sure-- we are going to fall down. Maybe we will break an ankle.

The large-scale swing set looks dangerous and forbidding-- but we'll grow into it.

But look at all the new things to master. Does life get any better than facing all these new challenges? What _are_ we waiting for?

"What are you waiting for?"

Dr. Robert Wright, Principal, Mulberry Elementary School, Whittier, California

Library of Congress Control Number: 2010900371
ISBN-10: 1450507697
ISBN-13/EAN-13: 9781450507691